# THE
# WAR
# AS
# I SAW
# IT

D1569963

*Harvey L. Harris (1893–1955)*

# THE
# WAR
# AS
# I SAW
# IT

## 1918 LETTERS
## *of a*
## TANK CORPS
## LIEUTENANT

# HARVEY L. HARRIS

ISBN 1-880654-12-1

Library of Congress No. 97-75424

Book design by Will Powers
Typesetting by Stanton Publication Services, Inc.
Cover design by McLean & Tuminelly

# CONTENTS

# ACKNOWLEDGEMENTS

We wish to acknowledge the inspiration and assistance of two sisters of Harvey Harris. The first, Eleanor Harris, lovingly treasured and preserved his letters for nearly fifty years. She single-handedly managed to keep alive our interest in them. The second, Marilee H. Asher, along with her husband Bob, carefully reviewed the manuscript drafts and corrected them for facts which only they would know.

Rodney C. Loehr, retired professor of history at the University of Minnesota, read the letters, and strongly urged their publication. It was his recommendation that gave this project its final impetus. We cannot omit Frank Harris, the nephew of Harvey Harris to whom the letter quoted in the Preface was addressed, who provided on-going computer assistance and general encouragement. Thanks, also, to I. B. Holley, professor of history at Duke University, who read the letters and gave his comments.

Finally, we thank Aleth Depaz and Aurore de Laval and the Musée de l'Armée-Service Photographique, for the poster from which the front cover design was based, which is illustrated at page 72, and for the photographs at pages 54, 65, 85, 120, and 123; to Thérèse Blondet-Bisch and the Musée d'Histoire Contemporaine (BDIC) for the photographs at page 104, and 128; to the Bibliothèque Forney, for the post card illustrated at page xiii; to Libby Chenault and the Rare Book Collection, University of North Carolina, for the poster from which the back cover design was based, illustrated at page xii, and the poster at page 38; to the Liberty Memorial Museum, for the poster illustrated at page 59; and to Thomas E. Reiersgord for the June 13, 1918 envelope, postmarked at Gettysburg, Pennylvania, carrying the Tank Corps logo. This logo was used to enhance each chapter heading.

We are grateful to all for their assistance on this project.

# PREFACE

Nearly twenty-seven years after the Armistice ended the "War to End All Wars," Harvey Louis Harris wrote a letter to his nephew, then about to enlist in the army for service in World War II. He reminisced about his service in World War I. He pointedly recalled the advice of his Battalion commander, Lt. Colonel (later General) George S. Patton, Jr., given while he served in the Meuse-Argonne offensive: "I suppose some of you men are fighting to make this world free. I'm not! I am in it because I just like it, that's all." Harris apparently agreed. He went on to say to his nephew, "you are going to have more fun and sport than you ever had!" And he concluded, "In 20 years you'll say it was the most interesting experience you've ever had." In short, based upon his mid-western instincts and middle-class orientation, war was a game to Harris.

Born in Chicago in 1893, Harvey Harris attended University High School, the laboratory school of the University of Chicago. His father, Frank, was one of the principals in the Chicago House Wrecking Company, the firm which wrecked the facilities and cleared the grounds of the 1893 World's Columbian Exposition, as well as the St. Louis World's Fair of 1904. As a part of their salvage work the company purchased the well-known Ferris Wheel, and later operated it at the St. Louis World's Fair of 1904. Harvey Harris had one brother, Francis (who also served in World War I, and is referred to in the letters as "Babe"), and three sisters, Imogene, Eleanor, and Marilee (nicknamed "Buns" in the letters.) The family resided in the Hyde Park neighborhood of the south-side of Chicago.

In 1906, when Harris was 13 years old, he accompanied his parents on a Grand-Tour-of-Europe, visiting France, England, and Belgium. He kept a diary and carefully penned a number of letters back to his sisters. This was to be good practice for the writing of his war-time letters.

On this trip Harris had his first glimpse of Paris, and he learned a bit about French language and culture. France was to fascinate him a dozen years later when he was an officer in the American Expeditionary Force. Harris made at least one other trip to France (in 1921) when he took time to visit the battlefields where he had seen action and the cemetery at Verdun.

In 1914 Harvey Harris graduated from the University of Chicago as a geology-major. In his senior year he earned All-Western conference honors as a guard on the 1913 championship football team, led by the legendary coach, Amos Alonzo Stagg. Along with many of his fellow graduates Harris entered the military service shortly after the April 6, 1917 declaration of war by the United States against Germany. Following the prescribed officer's candidate training of approximately 90 days, he obtained a commission as second-lieutenant, artillery, at Fort Sheridan, Illinois.

Harris and about 1,200 other troops and civilians embarked on March 31, 1918, for Europe on *Le Rochambeau*, a French-Line steamship being used for military transportation. "No trip could be more enjoyable," he commented. "The scotch was plentiful and the food excellent. . . . Just four items: a soup, meat, vegetable and fromage or fruit— but those frogeaters could cook. The darndest pleasure trip I ever took. Merveilleux!"

Successively, in France, Harris served as a supply or utility officer in charge of truck-trains carrying wagons or caissons, and of troop trains, loading, unloading and provisioning the soldiers on board. On occasion he was in charge of the horses in ammunition trains. For a short time, also, he was the military provost-marshal of the area, in which he was charged with the disciplining of drunken soldiers. In short, he functioned much like Pooh-Bah (Lord High Everything Else) in *The Mikado*, an operetta by Gilbert & Sullivan. The ability of Harris, then only 25 years of age, to handle such diverse tasks efficiently and promptly clearly caught the attention of his superior officers.

During most of the war both sides utilized armored cars. However, these vehicles were essentially road-bound. During September of 1916 a techno-military breakthrough occurred. Armored cars with treads, popularly known as "tanks," first saw action with the British army in France. Employed in large formations, these tanks were particularly useful in breaching barbed-wire entanglements and crossing trenches,

destroying machine-gun nests and blockhouses and, in general, sup-
porting the infantry. Shortly thereafter the French and, later on, the
German armies began to utilize tanks as well. It was commonly believed at the time that, in addition to the airplane, the tank would certainly help the Allies win the war.

At about the same time the United States Army also began to consider tank-technology. A large tank training-camp was established in
Camp Colt, near Gettysburg, Pennsylvania, under the command of
Major Dwight D. Eisenhower. Men from every other arm of the military service turned eagerly to the Tank Corps. According to the *Chicago
Tribune*, "hundreds of prosperous and successful leaders in civil life are
swarming to the fighting colors of the tanks and are striving to emu-
late in their pugnacious aggressiveness the snarling wildcat that has
been chosen as the emblem of the tank service. Take them all in all,
physically, mentally, and culturally, the tank men are declared to be the
flower of the Army." By the end of the war, in fact, the Tank Corps had
grown from 500 men to a significant new fighting force of some 10,000
enlisted men and 600 officers. It was little wonder, then, that Harvey
Harris urgently desired to join the Tank Corps.

*Post card showing the British heavy tank, MK1, which weighed 28 tons and carried
a crew of eight. It was 26 feet 5 inches long, had a maximum speed of 4.6 M.P.H.
and a range of 25 miles. British tanks were first used in battle on July 15, 1916.*

*Recruiting poster for the Tank Corps, with its*
*"Wanted: Husky Young Americans . . ." appeal.*
From the copy in the Rare Book Collection,
University of North Carolina at Chapel Hill

Harris expressed his reasons quite simply for seeking a transfer to the Tank Corps:

1. The wonderful possibilities of the Tank
2. The desire for blood (grrrr)
3. The fact that I would have a hand in it from its inception. Practically among the first in the Tank Corps of the U.S.— a unique and desirable situation
4. And, I admit, the romance of such a service which is a combination of all branches.

By early June, 1918, Harvey Harris became a tank officer at the 301st Tank Center, at Bourg, near Paris. This facility had been established by Colonel (later Brigadier General) Samuel D. Rockenbach to familiarize American Expeditionary Force personnel with tanks and tank warfare. Harris was first assigned as a driving instructor. "I like to just be around those darn little things, just like around horses. Certainly is fascinating. Especially when you always have subconscious knowledge of what they can do, their potentiality." Harris enjoyed his work: "I am in charge of all driving now. . . . It keeps one humping all morning.

3. - Chars Renault en terrain accidenté.

*Two Renault tanks are shown in difficult terrain. French tanks made their first appearance in the battle of the Somme (1916). In 1917 Jean-Baptiste Estienne developed the Schneider tank, using American tractor treads. Renault tanks with 37 mm. cannons were introduced in 1918.*
Post card courtesy of the Bibliothèque Forney, Paris.

When new men arrive they are put through instruction in all courses—machine gun, signalling, shop work, driving, etc. All have to qualify. Then they are assigned to companies. I take a bunch out every morning and that field is as busy as a jazz band dance. Scurrying around, up and down, about the most pleasant work of 'em all."

The French Renault light tank which Harris drove was 16 feet 5 inches long, weighed 7.4 tons, and had armor plate between 0.3 and 0.6 inches thick. With a maximum speed of 6 miles per hour, and a 39 horsepower engine, the tank had a range of 24 miles. Crewed by a driver and a gunner, it had either a 37 mm. cannon or an 8 mm. machine gun mounted in a fully traversing turret. American-built tanks, incidentally, were not available until after the war had ended.

Harris was commissioned a first Lieutenant in the Tank Corps on July 18, 1918. By the middle of August, 1918, there were fifty officers and nine hundred fully trained men at the Bourg Tank center.

For Harris, war was a game. On August 5, 1918, General Harry A. Smith, accompanied by his military aide, and by Julius Rosenwald, President of Sears, Roebuck & Company,[1] visited the camp at Langres, where Harris was giving instruction in tank driving. Addressing the General, Harris said, "Sir, is it your wish to have a tank manoeuvre for Mr. Rosenwald?" The General replied in the affirmative, "so I got my best sergeant and told him to take the shell holes, trenches and then hit for the woods—about 300 meters away. Damned if it didn't go swell, just like a circus horse and I felt like the trainer receiving the plaudits of the audience. . . . Just then the tank hit a tree at the edge of the woods, went up on end and then disappeared. 'He's tipped over,' yelled Mr. R. I said we'll go over and see. We went. Tipped over, Hell! It was moving thru, riding over stumps, trees, walls and everything. Then it backed out just as easily. 'A sight of a lifetime,' said Mr. J.R. and even the general got ecstatic."

Harris saw action as acting company commander of Company C, 345th Tank Battalion, which utilized the Renault light tanks. The two major campaigns in which Harris participated were the relatively mild action against the Germans at the St. Mihiel salient, near to the Meuse river, on September 12–14, 1918, and the major offensive at the Meuse-Argonne front, on September 26–28, 1918. The latter campaign was characterized by tough American fighting and savage German resistance.

Even after participating in these and other actions, Harris remained

Preface

XV

convinced that the Tank Corps was the place to be. "Why I'm just nuts about it—Jules Verne's, *20,000 Leagues under the Sea* or Aviation are as naught B4 us—as the good Einhorn's prayer book says. There'll be more romance connected with this service than—say—Horatio Alger could write about."

A heavy smoker for his entire life, Harris was especially proud of a silver cigarette case with a rough indentation in the center. Due to limited visibility to the front, it was often customary for an officer to lead his platoon of tanks into battle. The cigarette case was in Harris' shirt pocket and, in the course of his leading such a tank platoon, had deflected a German bullet! The case undoubtedly had saved his life. Harris was exceptionally lucky. By October 4, 1918, fifty-three percent of the officers of his unit, the 1st Tank Brigade (including the Brigade commander, four of six captains, and twelve of the twenty-four lieutenants) and sixty-five enlisted men (twenty-five percent) were either dead or wounded.

Harris had a clear and concise way with writing. One of his reports was published in *Treat 'Em Rough*,[2] and was cited in a major biography of General Patton.[3] Another of his reports of Tank Corps action was published in a Chicago newspaper. Entitled "Our Tanks in Battle: Adventure of American Platoons," it provides some of the flavor of his battle experiences:

> Our jumping off point was on a plateau, about 50 feet above the valley we were in. When the artillery opened up at about 5:20 A.M. we started out. It would take us ten minutes to get there with the infantry. As we went up the hill it grew lighter and I distinguished the support infantry in shallow trenches standing at their machine guns and putting over a barrage, every gun shooting at will and as fast as the belts could be put in.
>
> The barrage of the Boches grew heavier as soon as the tanks came over the hill. My first distraction from checking up to see if my fifteen tanks were all there and going well was when I almost tripped over a wounded doughboy lying on the ground.
>
> I've never seen a more terrible yet more wonderful counterbarrage than the one the Boche laid down as we advanced that morning. Not 77's but 105's to 240's. And as regular as could be. As we advanced the range dropped and the shells fell always right in our line. I'll bet I spent half that morning falling desparately and then getting up again.

The [tank] platoons scattered out for their different objectives, or to help infantry which were held up somewhere. I could see them scattered on both sides of me—some stationary and probably firing at a machine gun, others out of action with their crews crawling out to make hasty repairs, still others stopped and their doors closed, perhaps a direct hit and both of the crew bumped off. One or two stuck in holes at uncomfortable angles.

During a lull a tank lieutenant got a glimpse of one of our tank commanders—a sergeant—coming back. He was ashen white against the black leather helmet he wore. The lieutenant went over to see what ailed him. Here's the story: This sergeant was a gunner with a corporal driving. They were going through some heavy brush when he felt the tank sinking away from him. They went down for what he imagined was fifteen feet or more, and while slipping the tank was turning over on its side. The water began pouring in the slits. The driver couldn't open his front door on account of the weight of water and mud. When they realized they were overturned and submerged the driver said: 'We both can't make it. You get out.' The sergeant managed to open the back door and get out. The driver was drowned. Then no sooner was this sergeant out than our doughboys, thinking he was a German, began firing at him.

By this time we were coming down the valley southwest of Exermont. The sides go up forty or fifty feet.

The tanks were to rally at Exermont in the afternoon, and we had to get there—1,000 yards away. From here on things got more intricate.

Sitting in a shellhole I sent back word as to our location and what the situation looked like, then started on. We were getting into a hot bed. Careful listening told us there were at least three machine guns ahead. We probably wouldn't have gone on if we had stopped to think. It's best not to. Soon we were out in an open plain. It was becoming a madhouse. Possibly 200 shots a minute were being fired at us. We hadn't noticed any other troops for half an hour.

Things were looking a 'leetle' bad. There was a slight rise of ground twenty yards ahead and a ring of loose earth. It was our only chance.

We played and won. Never have I seen a more beautiful sight. One by one we went into it—seal fashion. Its sides were as smooth as if done by hand. And eight feet deep. Think of the comfort of standing up! Nothing but a direct hit would bother us now.

We saw a lieutenant and two men crawling near by, and yelled for them to come in. No wonder we were so royally treated with machine gun and boche artillery. Our front line was half a kilometer back, and they had nothing else to attract their attention.

After two hours and forty-five minutes we decided to duck back, make a quick rush of it. Just a chance we'd all get by unhit. But not a shot came.

On the weekends, war took a holiday for the officers. According to one of Harris' letters, "we were at the Grand Hotel [in Paris] and I gradually remembered little things dating back to '06. Our schedule was a late breakfast and then a front seat in front of the Cafe de la Paix. It is wonderful there. Everybody passes by or stops for a drink. Hardly ten minutes go by without seeing a friend. I met fellows continually—that I knew from high school days down to those I have known in the service. And it is always—have a drink or another."

The life of an officer was not always spent on one of the grand boulevards of Paris. Following his return from the front, Harris wrote that he "had the first bath in two months yesterday. In a nice white porcelain tub—tile floor, and heavy bath mat. . . . The shock of hot water was almost fatal. In fact, any water, even on my face causes extreme agitation and squirming."

War was a game and for the winners there were trophies. "You should have seen this place a few hours ago . . ." one of Harris' letters said. "Everybody looking for souvenirs, left by Boche. Helmets, guns, boots, everything. One of our infantry companies which was in reserve was lined up in front of a Boche supply room outfitting itself. . . . The only thing I really wanted was a German pistol. Couldn't find one. Helmets, rifles, leather gas masks, bayonets, etc., etc. laying around. . . ." A German machine gun and other ordinance collected by Harvey Harris were donated by his family early in 1942 to the World War II scrap metal drive, thus perhaps returning these now rusty bits of weaponry to duty in a new European war.

There were souvenirs and there also was recognition. "Before I forget I want you to know that . . . we original Tankers have already been cited TWICE. Once by General Pershing, himself, and another by the General who was in command of the second show. Couched in won-

derful terms they are conducive to increased chest measurements, to
say the least. Other organizations are in same orders but Gen. Pershing's is a personal letter to our commanding general." That letter, to
General Rockenbach, was dated September 16, 1918. Harris was also recommended for the Distinguished Service Cross (D.S.C.) but his commanding general did not grant him this medal. Harris would have ap-
proved of the lyrics in *Mademoiselle from Armentiers*, a popular song of
those war years:

> *Yes the General got the Croix de Guerre*
> *But the sonofabitch was never there!*
> *Hinkey—Dinkey—Parley Vous.*

But the hoped-for promotion to captain eluded him; the Armistice
came before the paperwork could be processed. Yet, Harris wrote,
"Look at the bright side! I have been up in the line for 2 months—in 2
big shows—with the fightingest branch in the service—in an outfit
cited twice and still raring to go. That's worth more. N'est-ce pas?"

War was a game, but it had to end. "My days of excitement are
over—if there is an armistice. I am not a glutton. I had a couple of
months of the real thing—and there are so many who are raring to go.
But it is wonderfully exciting. There is nothing to compare with an
army attack—the preparation—it's more than exhilarating. One can't
get the same feelings from anything else."

Following the war Harris organized and was general manager of the
housing division of Sears, Roebuck & Company. This division sold
ready built or pre-fabricated housing. Between 1937 and 1941 he served
as the site manager for the construction in Ogallala, Nebraska of the
Kingsley-Keystone Dam, then the largest earth-filled dam in the world.
He eventually owned and operated a model 13,000 acre cattle ranch in
Sterling, Colorado, where he became an authority on erosion control,
cloud seeding, and range grasses. Harris died September 18, 1955, and is
buried in Chicago.

The corpus of this book contains forty-six letters from France
which Harris wrote to his mother and father (familiarly called "Mater"
or "Ma Cherie," and "Pater," respectively) and to his siblings and aunts,
between the end of February, 1918 and the end of January, 1919. Upon
receipt by the family the letters were transcribed by typewriter and

shared with many other relatives and friends. His use of fractured French, slang, and the so-called Dewey spelling, with words such as "thot," "mite," "frinstance," and "B4," and other similar abbreviations in the letters, has not been edited. While Harris, as an officer, censored his own letters, his decision as to what information to impart was clearly made so as not to worry his family. Our principal editing of the letters was to remove a number of personal, family references, and to insert, parenthetically, the identification of named individuals, and the interpretation of military terminology and various slang terms.

The letters of Harvey Harris are important for a number of reasons. They are well-written, informative, humorous and lucid. Few such first-person letters from Tank Corps personnel during World War I have been published. The letters show Harris' personal attitude towards war and all of its ramifications. For the military historian they bring out the confusion in the management of the American Expeditionary Force, and the absence of sound staff work, which is reflected in the continual change of orders. They also indicate that Harris was a conscientious young officer who took his military responsibilities seriously.

The publication of the Harvey Harris letters is intended to coincide with the 80th anniversary of the November 11, 1918 Armistice, which ended World War I. It has been stated, with some justification, that historians have virtually ignored the American experience with tanks in the first World War.[4] This book is not meant to be the last word in World War I tank history or strategy, for that has already been written by military historians. Rather, it is a window upon the experiences of one man in a fascinating but short period in American military history.

For Lieutenant Harvey Harris war was much like the football games he had played in. World War I for him was a challenge, a fast-moving, bold adventure which lasted little more than eighteen months. Harris had survived the bad times, savored the good, and returned home uninjured. His family vicariously shared these experiences through the many letters home. Harris had joined the army whose participation in what was called the "War to End All Wars" was hopefully understood and enthusiastically supported by most Americans.[5] That feeling was perhaps best expressed in the words of George M. Cohan's well-known song, *Over There*:

*So prepare, say a prayer,*
*Send the word, send the word to beware,*
*We'll be over, we're coming over,*
*And we won't come back till*
*It's over over there.*

Harris was surely mindful of such ideology and thinking. Yet, as an adventure he sought, obtained, and gloried in, a small but important role in the new military world of tanks. That was what Harris was to remember for the rest of his life.

As Samuel Hynes wrote in his study of soldiers' narratives, "but for ordinary men—the men who fight our wars—there will probably be only that one time when their lives intersect with history, one opportunity to act in great events . . . to be there, in history."[6] In the long run, however, and more important than the camaraderie of military life or the opportunity to experience the new tanks, Harvey Harris was "Over There," in the "War to End All Wars," and his letters were as a lens, focusing upon a small bit of history for his family. That is why they are published here.

LEO J. HARRIS
St. Paul, Minnesota
October 17, 1997

# NOTES TO THE PREFACE

1. In the early months of the war Rosenwald was head of the Committee on Supplies, which helped the Army's Quartermaster Corps procure military hardware and equipment. He was presumably visiting France in this capacity.

2. 1st Lt. Harvey L. Harris, Personal Experience Report, 19 Dec. 1918, Patton Military Papers, Box 47, Personal Experience Reports of Tank Operations—1918, Patton Collection, as published in Dale E. Wilson, *Treat 'Em Rough! The Birth Of American Armor*, 1917–1920. Novato, California: Presidio Press, 1989, pp. 154–155. The Report is also reprinted in the Appendix to this book.

3. Carlo D'Este. *Patton. A Genius for War.* New York: HarperCollins Publishers, Inc., 1995, p. 65, note 68.

4. Wilson, *op. cit.*, p. ix.

5. Military historian Rodney C. Loehr points out America entered this war, as it entered World War II, to restore the balance of power in Europe. For the ordinary citizen, however, the morale-boosting reason was to restore democracy in Europe. For Harvey Harris, a conservative and a sceptic, that became the restoration of Europe for the democrats.

6. Samuel Hynes. *The Soldiers' Tale. Bearing Witness to Modern War.* New York: Viking Penguin, 1997, p. 2.

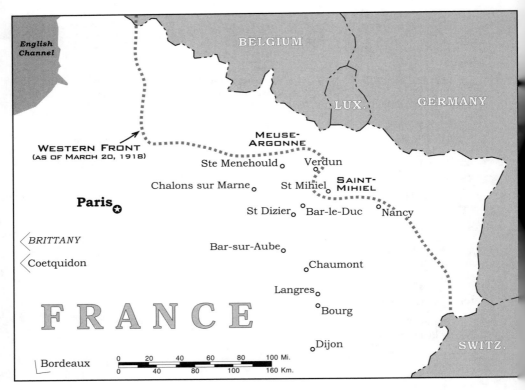

*Map of France, showing particular areas referred to in the letters.*

# 1

## AT SEA
## AND
## IN TRANSIT

TANK CORPS

TREAT EM' ROUGH

*At Sea*
*Le Rochambeau*
*March 30, 1918*

DEAR FOLKS,

It was a great nite. I got back at 2 o'clock A.M. and went over to the orderly room: Sykora [Anton Sykora, Batavia, Illinois] had been working all the time. We kept at it, checking service records, revising lists etc., until 4 o'clock. Then I took a turn in the bed that was in the room until 5:30. It's a great life if you don't weaken, I'll tell the world.

Then this morning: Have you ever had to do something absolutely compelled to—at a definite time—and it always seems impossible? Not a chance in the world to do it. That was this morning. We had a definite hour to depart and until we actually got there (only 10 minutes late) I said to myself 100 times, if once, "Christ, if we miss that train."

But we're on board now and I suppose you are waiting to hear from me. Not a chance. A fine big boat with Syk and myself sharing a 4 berth stateroom. Just like we were going over on pleasure.

The only L of it is: All the boat crew including waiters etc. are "frog-eaters" and I can see a wonderful time ahead trying to get special food, etc.

Most remarkable of all—we have our full quota stowed away on board. No more A.W.O.L's for awhile, at any rate.

There is a very interesting crowd on board: Canadian soldiers—Poles—French and quite a few French people.

I don't know when the mail is to be collected so will post this right away.

I don't see how anyone can worry when you see the little girls, etc., and families on board. "Just as safe as a baby playing with a loaded revolver."

The satisfactory part of the whole thing is that we've put away another job correctly. And it was a beaner, if I get time I'm going to try and describe it adequately.

And now—Don't Worry. I am able to handle the situation whatever it may be.

You'll hear from me as often as possible—and remember this: consider no word equal to a daily cable that I'm O.K.

With fondest love to all and wishes for early and successful culmination of this jaunt.

*Harv*

Whoopee—After 8 months! Better than my first long pants.

*Tuesday Morning*
*April 2, 1918*
*On Board Le Rochambeau*

This is the most wonderful trip I ever imagined one could have. In the first place the weather can't be beaten, balmy spring and the sea! as smooth as the Chicago River after a garbage boat or chop suey boat has passed. I have been trying to "shoot the sun" and keep dope on our course.

For the first 15 hours or from 4 o'clock Saturday, when we left, until about noon Sunday, and Easter Sunday at that, we were going north, probably up around Halifax. Since then always south-east.

The dope is we go to Bordeaux so our route will probably be way south towards the Canary Islands and then up thru the Bay of Biscay. (I don't know where that is, but some ladies-to-wear merchant said so).

He further states (he is Mr. Lowenthal who has stores in Paris and New York and formerly in Berlin) that he has knowledge that we will be the first troops to arrive at that port and we will probably get a wonderful welcome. It might be wonderful but I dread to think how we will show up—190 men but no organization at all.

Damned if our military experience hasn't been as varied as it has been interesting! Especially Bud's, Syk's and mine. Haven't had a chance to get bored with any one assignment before being put on another. Take mine for instance. The first 3 weeks in Chickamauga Park with Motor Truck Co. 2, organizing all the misfits and cast-offs transferred to us by other regiments. Then a month as Asst. Adjutant to Colonel Hunt, telling regular army Majors where to head in, and in the meanwhile talking football to the "Old Man" himself. He's a Michigan fan and when Chicago beat Michigan in basketball (the first meeting since that football game) I blue-pencilled the account—that broke the ice.

If anyone were to say to me with tears in his eyes, "My boy, you are doing a wonderful thing. Making a big sacrifice and rite in the full bloom of your youth—going out to war and very likely never to return"—I'd tell him to go to 'ell—that he was crazy as a bat.

Some of the officers really believe they are going to war. So far on this trip there hasn't been a single indication of it. Exactly the same kind of trip we had in 1906. Promenaders continually whirling by. Little children and old women out on deck. Dancing in the Salon nites, the piano always going. I had a few too many scotches last night to describe adequately how I feel—but imagine the best trip you ever made across and this one has it beaten 100 ways.

If it weren't for the uniforms the war might have been over for years. There is very little talk about the war or submarines, either.

I understand we will not be convoyed [escorted by navy anti-submarine vessels]. This ship never has. Still this is the first time she has carried American troops. That might make it necessary. Dope has it, also, this is the last passenger trip she will make—then U. S. transport. It's a swell boat.

Besides our men, there are some 250 waterworks engineers and some 5 engineer officers. I believe we two are the senior line officers on the boat, altho Capt. Stickney of the engineers is in command while on the boat.

In all there are 1200 troops on board. The balance of 6–700 are Poles going over to join French army. They were in training at Fort Niagara and about six Polish officers are with them. We had only one man on sick report this A.M. and I don't believe there are 5 men under the weather among all the troops.

Howard Woodhead [A neighbor in Chicago] in a Y.M.C.A. uniform ran into me the first day. He is going to work in the French army. Out of 100 "Ymers" most are going to work with the French and from where I stand I believe their work is cut out . They had one week of lectures on French habits and customs at Princeton and they are butchering French all the way. Now how in 'ell they are going to get any response from trench-weary French soldiers is more than I can gather. A number are $900 preachers from empty mudhole. But they mean well, I suppose. The richest part of it is that several of the brethren have been imbibing in the salon, and playing poker, and some sky pilot has tried to "work on" them and they told him where to head in. You see some few are real guys—businessmen—who wanted to do something and will do executive or accountant work on the other side.

We are more than half way—It's almost this side now.

Mr. Vincent, formerly of the U. of C.—later of U. of Minn., is also a passenger. [George Edgar Vincent, professor of sociology at the University of Chicago, then president of the University of Minnesota. He became head of the Rockefeller Foundation in 1917.] Woodhead introduced me, and he said he remembered me. He is going over for some six weeks, I suppose in connection with welfare work.

*On Land (Bordeaux)*
*April 10, 1918*
*in France*

MA CHERI (PLURAL?),

Voila! At last over here in a rest camp situated in the most beautiful country that I could ever imagine. I've seen paintings—being quite an art student—that I imagined were idealistic—impossible—but honestly I could rave on indefinitely. How anyone can go into ecstasies over such holes as Lake Geneva, Adirondacks or the Hudson is beyond me.

Le « Rochambeau » paquebot destiné au transport des passagers de 2ᵉ et 3ᵉ classes du Havre à New-York. Longueur 163 m., largeur 19 m. 40, profondeur 13 m. 20, tirant d'eau 8 m. 18, déplacement 17.300 tonnes. Ce paquebot est construit en acier, a 4 ponts couplés, il est muni de 2 machines alternatives et de 2 à turbines actionnant ensemble 4 hélices. La puissance de ses machines est de 11.000 chevaux, la vitesse de 19 nœuds. Le bateau peut recevoir 1.884 passagers et 400 hommes d'équipage, ce qui fait un total de 2.284 âmes. Il est muni des appareils de télégraphie sans fil à longues distances qui lui permettent de rester pendant toute la traversée en communication avec l'Europe ou l'Amérique.

51   *LE HAVRE.* — Le « Rochambeau », de la Cie Générale Transatlantique. — LL.

*According to the postcard text, the C.G.T. or French Line steamship,*
Le Rochambeau, *usually carried passengers between Le Havre and New York.*
*In April, 1918 Lt. Harris and 1,200 other American troops*
*travelled to Bordeaux aboard this vessel.*

I never was able to, but when we started up a river yesterday morning and saw villas, and hog sheds—the latter of which resembled our millionaires' garages. And yet it was all just plain farming country. Trays beans, [Tres bien, very good] Edie! Mater, when this little show is over, you come over here and I'll be satisfied to spend considerable time just walking around.

And even at that I haven't seen a thing as we only got in at 10 last nite and it's noon now, and the farthest I have walked is from our quarters to the men's barracks.

I mite have written a letter on the boat and you would have heard from me perhaps a day or two earlier, but I'm glad I didn't because I feel like "poeming" this morning. You no doubt have got the postals I mailed B4 we left and my cable sent to the office on arrival. I just looked up "So why worry" in a soldier's French Dictionary that a Beautiful actress gave me on shipboard but there's evidently no such idiom. Incidentally she claims she starred with Mrs. Fiske and others and we discussed plays and players at great length. Maybe we did.

The trip over was wonderful. You'll be surprised to hear that I wasn't sick a minute, and I don't believe it was the Calomel [A white, tasteless powder used as a cathartic for worms!] entirely (altho that mite have helped). The sea was like a small lake the entire way except for a few hours. No trip could be more enjoyable. The scotch was plentiful and the food excellent. Very much different from the menus we had on the *Carmania* years ago. Just 4 items: a soup, meat, vegetable and fromage or fruit—but those frogeaters could cook. The damndest pleasure trip I ever took! Merveilleux!

Howard Woodhead, Mr. Vincent, Mrs. Herrick [wife of the American Ambassador to France, Myron Herrick], and other Chicagoans were aboard and a lot of Red Cross and Y.M. girls. So you can see it mite have been an interesting trip. Woodhead got on in "civs" [civilian clothes] and I sort of recognized him—then a little later he bumped into me in his Y.M.C.A. khaki. There were a few other officers aboard and we are still with them, but they have orders now. Suppose we'll get ours directly.

As you have probably gathered from the above our method of travel over was entirely different than I ever imagined which, of course, made it much more "intrikate," and even at that until the last 36 hours you might have looked "all over 'ell" and you'd never imagine a thing other than a peace-time jaunt. Even the last day—except for some weak sisters among our Y.M.C.A. males—you couldn't find or see a life-belt. I didn't even find mine until the last day and it wasn't because I'm so brave but because of the whole general feeling prevalent. Of course, rumors were and are rife about our narrow escapes, etc., but of course, everyone knew their boat number. I mite also mention in passing that there was no delay at all when we left and no excitement except of course when the old Statue of Liberty moved by.

It was a great life—sleep until 8:30 or so, have our "Louie" bring in coffee—that rotten French stuff—no cream—and dry bread—but it was enuf to work thru a licouce (liquorish) mouth so one could at least talk.

The rest of the morning was put in promenading, attending to some military matters—with arms and Sam Browne belt. Tres Jollie!

Well, one morning we found ourselves anchored out in some river mouth and spent the next hours in docking finally but mostly in rhapsodical statements about the landscape—answering cheers from the shores with every whistle going full tilt as we passed. Very exciting.

How is everyone? Certainly hope your throat is better, Mater, and that you will all keep full of pepper, wim and wigor. Has Babe left for Custer yet? Gosh darn, this is wonderful! In France at last and just between us girls, we're not going to be here at this camp much longer.

Mail should be addressed to me c/o 3rd Ammunition Train A.E.F., via New York. Maybe I'll get some of it. And don't worry.

*Best love,*
*Harv*

*April 11, 1918*

DEAR MATER:
I am going to continue my letter of this A.M. and try and give you an idea of some of the interesting things I've seen and done because we are very likely to get ordered away from here tomorrow—in which case it may be a week B4 I'll get another opportunity.

Yes, yes, we're listening! Well it's now 10:30 P.M. Since 3 this afternoon I've been censoring mail. Well, just imagine the number of men we have and consider they have been here 2 days with nothing to do and it means reading every word. And there are only two officers. Without exception, all are nuts over the beauties of this country and many descriptions are so wonderful I really am ashamed. One man wrote, "To attempt to describe the wonderful beauties is to insult them." A lot of them are funny too.

Last nite, I spent in Bordeaux, i.e., until 10 P.M. It's a great lively town. I went in with another Lieut. and we sat out in front of a cafe, (you know, out on the sidewalk) and sipping our beers—we're allowed beer and light wine until 8:30. We watched the people go by. Every kind of uniform and a lot of beautiful women, most of whom are more beautiful than righteous or hesitant. Tres Mal! Degoutant! [Disgusting.] But you need not worry. I'm in this thing now, as a military man. As far as the enlisted man is concerned the M.P. watch him pretty close.

But from the little I've seen and heard—and I admit it has only been a "Little"—this is no place for young American girls to do Canteen or War work. Mature women, yes, but the younger girls can accomplish more under better conditions in the States.

I said above we mite get our "movement" orders. I've reconsidered that and believe it O.K. to say we have them and after we two take the men one place we are ordered to proceed to another. Very likely the former is our outfit. If the latter, we find, is not promising—we'll work on the Colonel. Maybe, tho, it might be the place I've wanted to go to.

So far camps here are the same as in the States and there's no inconvenience in getting almost anything but sweets. In every letter I censored today the men gave hints to sweethearts, strong suggestions to friends and orders to relatives concerning same. But I'm in swell shape, 1500 cigarettes, 1 box of Pater's cigars, some chocolate cached away in different places.

And say, an American officer is some guy at least with Uncle Sam. I mean by that, as you have probably also noticed, that one is treated very excellently. Frinstance, we not only got a trip over here, but even a little thing like tips! There is a special voucher for them. As a result I got $10 for what I paid out, including even a steamer chair that some Y.M. playmate commandeered the first day after which it was never again seen.

As I have told Babe [Francis, Harris' younger brother, who was stationed at Nevers] time and time again: "Get a sergeancy, work 24 hours a day if you have to, but get it." He's an officer without a commission but the gap is awfully big between a sergeant's warrant and a mere private. Impress this on him.

This letter is getting pretty much mixed up and I suppose it'll be ruddled [marked with red, for emphasis] by the assembled guests, but it's just an attempt by a poor, honest movie writer to cop off a little change.

There are so many I would like to write to! But it looks as tho my time for a week or more will be pretty well taken up. You might pass on the good word to anyone you meet. Call up Howell Murray [a college friend], frinstance and in general let the whole world know "that this is the place to be."

If I could be sure, Mater, Pater, et al, that you wouldn't be worrying because you don't hear, maybe for 3 or 4 weeks at a time, that you will always realize under field conditions mail gets lost, sunk etc. then I'd feel a lot better.

Gosh, it's darned near 12 P.M. Tres tard (oh, your little pocket dictionary is a wonder, Mater). And I've got to censor this yet—this mess which is without a doubt the worst I had today.

Au Revoir, ma chere famille.

*With lots of love,*
*Harv*

*April 13, 1918*
*On a train Somewhere near*
*Somewhere, in France*

DEAR FOLKS,

It's still a dream to me and I'll describe my present situation and you'll understand. Here we are moving up to a certain place, where we will hear the battle at least by tomorrow night. Syk and myself with a velour upholstered, 1st class compartment to ourselves. I just laid down Gerards' *My Two Years in Germany*, and Syk was reading some light novel. You know these side loader compartments. We've picked up food—a few hard boiled eggs—some russet apples—besides our travel rations,—and this, with our shaving outfits, towels, grips, old bedrolls (because we slept here last nite and will tonite), pistols, cigarettes, etc. up on the racks—it looks like we mite be two gout patients going to some "baths," or else just about to arrive at Manitowish, when Pater says, "You take care of the baggage—I'll go ahead." And honestly there is a stream out there now that is identical with the Flambeau. That gives you my frame of mind, about as much military as Marilee's, and yet I say tomorrow nite may give us our first introduction to "Big Bertha" [Largest of the German heavy cannon, made by Krupp, capable of shooting its 238 lb. shells as far as 90 miles] and we don't even kno unless we concentrate that there's a war going on. We might get the "Buck fever" later, and probably will, but what the 'ell boys!

You should have seen me this morning standing at the door of my compartment while in a large R. R. station, shaving! About as likely as doing it in the lobby of the Auditorium (I should have said, "apropos"). Syk snapped me. I hope it turns out good.

For a fact, I thot a lot more about the war before I got here. (There he goes again. He needs another shot.) and I can readily understand what I've heard (damn that flat wheel) that it's a business—just like going to the office every morning or eating regularly. I must have acquired that necessary spirit. Voila—a seasoned veteran.

My French is still inaccurate—not withstanding my long stay here already. But sometimes I can get by, and at other times my mouth stays open—can't even get a word out. You see I have to arrange for coffee at meal hours; so far we've always had it. So that shows I'm getting by. It's hard for a lot of these "birds" to down it, but they might as well get used to it. Just black—and unsweetened! I suppose Mr. Crowe, of U. Hi, [English teacher of Harris] would have a lot to say about my use of the dash (-) also n'est-ce pas?

Say, I've just read this thing, If you don't agree with me that it's the worst hieroglyphic and most disgusting jumble you ever saw—I'll set 'em up.

We were at the rest camp until yesterday afternoon, I wrote my first letter from there. I believe it is 150 miles from where the men I met in New York are stationed, and almost due South also from where Mann is.

Say, as I have often said my assignment as "utility officer" for the last 3 months has been the "nuts" if anything could be. In fact I've been in charge of (instead of "under") for so long I even argue with my superiors now. Wonderful experience! First Asst. to Adj., then in charge of Truck Train at Chickamauga [Fort Oglethorpe, Georgia], equipped it for service, and if I do say it—it was the best and most completely equipped of any outfit I've seen since as regards marking of equipment, fireless cookers, etc. Then Asst. Supply officer for the Trains, loading its machines and baggage. Meat officer on way to New York.

And then just as my baggage was being loaded for moving over here the next day—to get orders by orderly: "Will remain and bring over casuals."

Ten days more of Supply officer—equipping some 800 casuals for my division. Since then in charge of bringing men from U. S. to the Front (perhaps) with all concomitant (I don't often get a chance to use one like that) details and duties, loading, checking, boat drills, scurrying for food on our arrival at camp at 13 P.M. etc., etc. Then travel on French Railroads! It's too much! An experience in 4 months that in peace times one wouldn't get in 40 years in our past military history. It's too bad he is so conservative and bashful!

Now comes the most perplexing part of all! We are to take the men to our present ordered destination and upon being relieved to report to another place a considerable distance away. Why or how I don't know. Don't know whether our outfit is at former or latter place. But we'll see France, by gum! Write me c/o 3rd Ammunition Train until you hear otherwise. This is the life!

We pass U. S. Troops, now and then, and invariably one of our bucks yells, "Ride 'em, Cowboy." It sends the same sensation thru one that a 12 pound hungry "muskie" does. Imagine yourself where we are and have some bird yell that out at the top of his lungs. Very pleasing.

*April 14, 1918, 9 A.M.*

Going back over same road today. Last nite at about 11 P.M. after I had gone to sleep, i.e., dressed, but with that good old comforter around me, I was awakened by some loud English: "Where are the Ammunition Train officers?" I jumped up expecting some Boches [the French term for the Germans]—no, not at all. It was a 2nd Lt. in the QM. who had stopped our train. Our orders had been changed by wire, and luckily we were near a good sized town. We are now returning over a considerable part of the same road we came out over, ending up further north and very much nearer Mann's location than before. In other words, we were probably all wrong and have to return. We had wired ahead at 11 P.M. for coffee this A.M. expecting to continue on. Instead we had it where we had dinner yesterday. Don't know where our next coffee will be. Can't even figure that far ahead.


*April 16, 1918*

This is getting worse and worse—something like a honeymooner's diary—whatever that is like. But I mite as well bring this story up to and including our arrival at our destination—with the Ammunition Train, which was this afternoon at 4 P.M.

Imagine! From Friday 2 P.M. to Tuesday 4 P.M. living on the train—getting off at stations just long enuf to order or get coffee for the men. I only drew 3 days' of travel rations and we were moving 4 days. As soon as we were started back we couldn't get any information as to when we mite arrive not because of the great distances, but because of the hours spent with thee, dear sidetrack. 2 of the nites were spent that way. As a result it was a proposition of long waits between issues of grub. At best travel rations are not the most filling. So at 4 or 5 every afternoon the animals would begin begging for food. Just like a zoo—because we had guards on every car to keep the men from being left behind. We were resolved that we'd bring them all in. Some bird would yell out, "Who wants to eat?" and a deafening chorus would answer. In our compartment we'd sort of cringe like a mariner fearing a mutiny. Then some sweet voice—like a referee's at a prize fight would warble, "When do we eat, do you think we're actors?" Of course, not all addressed to, but most decidedly meant for us. Except for one or two meals at station restaurants we ate the same food.

From Sunday to Monday, last nite, we were moving. That's all—nothing exciting or particularly interesting. The country not nearly as picturesque or as much cultivated as further south—something like our Central and N. Central Wisconsin.

Yesterday afternoon we arrived at a place [in Brittany] only an hour from here—but no train until this afternoon. Swell prospects. While talking to the Chef de Gare, a French soldier who was standing by said, "Perhaps I can billet your men with my regiment." Syk went with him. And after the men had their coffee—about 9 P.M.—Syk returned successful. So we started the whole outfit down the narrow cobblestone streets to what was formerly a large convent, now used as billets for 10 times the men we had. Tray's beans, Eddie! Nice big mattresses, blankets and a place to stretch out. 8 in a compartment for 72 hours is not conducive to much rest, I'll tell the world! So at 11 P.M. we sought out a little French hotel—with a big courtyard and got fixed up very nicely. Then we started out to get food. Of course, everything was dark, the chimes in the big church nearby caused the only noise. Luckily 3 elderly gentlemen came along and we asked them in a Pure French where food could be had. One said, "Cafe Lion D'Or'" another said, "La Ferme." The 1st said, "Peut-etre pour Amerikan offitzer." So we walked with them a little ways and one knocked on a metal shutter, you know the kind that cover the whole store front. After giving the pass—we went in and sat down, the 3 Frenchmen sitting at a table nearby. The landlady brot some playing cards and one said to us, "This is a good excuse for us to stay out later." I immediately thot of the "solitaire" club, Pater, Maurie and Ben. We had 2 cups of coffee apiece, a big loaf of rye, 2 eggs up—both good and a glass of wine. 40 cents apiece. Very cheap, yes?

Our beds at the hotel were at first clammy and cold, indicating long uselessness. Withal, nice and clean. At eight this morning we were to meet the mayor of the town concerning permission to use some kitchen to cook a good hot meal, but at 8, a French corporal who travelled in England advised us he had already gotten permission and made arrangements. They certainly treat us fine!

We were to have mess cooked in a Catholic mission school. We made arrangements with a robed father, had our detail go into their old kitchen, containing old copper utensils—like I've imagined in monasteries, and at 11 A.M. the men had their first hot meal since leaving the Friday (previous).

At 1:30 we again entrained and from 2:30 to 4 were hiking from R. R. station to camp here [Coetquidon]. Our men were immediately distributed to the various companies. We reported to Lt. Colonel Lovell who was very much interested in our trip. Said he would take up the conflicting order I wrote about above and that we would be kept on Headquarters work, i.e., not assigned to any one company. That suits me fine, may have opportunities to make trips on special missions.

*Best love,*
*Harv*

# 2

# JACK
# OF ALL
# TRADES

TANK CORPS

TREAT EM' ROUGH

*Friday evening*
*April 19, 1918*

DEAR ONES,

There isn't anything of news to "carry on" where I left off in my last letter. I haven't done a heluva lot, either. You see, we got here Tuesday and as we were entitled to a couple days rest, this was really our first day of work. This morning we had some clerks getting up dope for us concerning QM and Ordnance property which we are charged up with at Merritt [Camp Merritt, New Jersey]—so we can pass on the charge, i.e., pass the buck of accountability to someone else. The haste in the States, you know, was great and the equipping of so many men with everything even down to shoe laces necessitated drawing and signing for 1000's of $ worth of equipment. Then after we had a number equipped they went A.W.O.L.—a few hours before we left, and we have nothing to show. Oh, it's a great life if you don't weaken! Some day when I'm 40 yrs. old or so I'll get a bill for this stuff and I'll have a fine chance of explaining.

I just happened to remember: I hastened out at a French station of a good sized town in S. Cent. France to arrange for coffee, and found a swell American Red Cross Bldg. and wonderful American girls running the canteen. The one in charge was very efficient; fixed up coffee and cocoa for all the men and furnished, besides, a clothes-basket of rye-bread sandwiches (charging 6 cents a cup for the whole thing). Well I got to talking with her. She was a U. of C. [University of Chicago] girl, class of '14. She pronounced her name 'Bergaher.' I believed it is spelled Berger. And she knew the Rosenwalds, Loebs [other neighbors], etc. We had a nice chat until the train pulled out.

I have a new assignment since yesterday and until—I don't know when: Headquarters Horse section, Ammunition Train. Ordinarily an assignment would start the letter, but no more! I'm too used to them, now. In other words instead of handling ammunition with trucks—the horse section carries wagons and caissons. If I'm in it very long I can join Ringley's Horseback Trio [possibly referring to an act in the Ringling Brothers- Barnum & Bailey circus.] N'est-ce pas?

*Sunday 6 P.M.*
*April 21, 1918*

Just had a pretty good supper at our officers' mess (hamburger, nice crisp lettuce, coffee and roquefort, nuts, soup) and I'm smoking a good old *El Sidelo* (the last of the first box Pater gave me). I was surprised at the quarters we have here, about as large as our back bedroom, a little renegade of a stove (that would keep a squad busy because it has no grate), two washstands of a strictly French type and trunks, suitcases, pitchers and clothes laying and hanging all over the room. Revolvers, spurs, haversacks and so on. It looks like a trappers' shack or a museum. It's great!

Beginning this morning I become a remount officer. This is along the lines of what Horse section does. I take care of enuf horses to move the town of Hyde Park on a busy May morning. Superintend feeding, watering, ministering to the sick, etc. It's very satisfying work. Out all day, no inside work; and I have a swell nag and just keep riding around. Of course, it is only temporary as some other outfit will happen along some day and be detailed on this work. When our equipment (freight) arrives we'll give the men a lot of equitation. In the meantime the other officers, with only 2 or 3 exceptions (Fossland's doing the same work as I am. Sykora is a supply officer) have to drill and lecture 7 to 8 hours a day. Almost the same schedule as at Fort Sheridan, and damned tiresome, I'll tell the world. I'm entirely satisfied with my job, but having tasted of the sea (i.e., have had so many assignments) I suppose I'll want a change after a month or so.

If ever a camp was run along strict, military lines, this one is. Officers stand every formation from reveille (5:45) to tattoo (8:36). No getting away even from the camp, unless on a military mission. I call it a beautiful desert. Only a few hours by truck from where Mann is frinstance. Something like scotch, scotch everywhere and not a drop to drink. You probably can infer that we are as far from the Front as is London and may be here several months. When we do go, tho, we auto be a real outfit. Mercer is with the M. P. up where we were originally scheduled for and probably doing duty. I knew the hookworm would get him! At one of the camps the Ammunition Train stopped en route here—he didn't like the layout, so went to a hotel. His outfit pulled out at nite on an hour's notice and he must have spent some wonderful morning when he finally returned after a shave and a leisurely break-fast! But he'll get by.

It's muggy and rainy here all day—in fact most of the time. This A.M. I found Buns' [the nickname of his little sister, Marilee] little gloves in my raincoat. Tell her I'll keep them for her and about 5 years after the war is over (i.e., when we get mustered out) will return them, status quo. Tres Bien, s'il vous plait!

There is an A. E. F. order out specifying a new kind of Kepi [military cap]. I'll send a picture some day. It's a beaner [Slang term meaning

*"If I don't look like an Algerian or French Sengalese I'm stuck for the drinks," Lt. Harris wrote to his mother on May 5, 1918, when he posed with his new kepi and Sam Browne belt. It is possible that the officer to the right was Captain Ranulf Compton, later commander of the 304th Tank Brigade's 345th Light Tank Battalion.*

something fine or excellent]. Like Harry Lauder's. If they're not any good for anything else they make a swell boudoir hat. Both Syk and I have them on now, tres Jollie!

Burns and I took a walk yesterday afternoon and ran into a little French town with 4 ft. thick stone walls on the Bldgs, one of those places you read about with horses, cows, children, pigs all running loose on the main street. As a result even a good American "white wing" [street cleaner] would have his work cut out. We wanted some figs and went into a little Epicerie [grocery store]. And we found another wedding going on, i.e., they were dancing. Two shuffles to the right, then 2 to the left, then repeat. After the dance each guy kisses his partner on both cheeks, and some one exclaims Ooh, la, la! A French soldier, evidently a great believer in war, was the groom.

I've seen 4 or 5 of my battery playmates from Fort Sheridan, who have just finished school over here, and stayed up to 12 one nite tearing the rag with one of them who spent 10 days up with a battery. Very interesting experience. Altho he claims he had several close calls, he said his feelings and the whole situation at the time, were as unimpressive as a crutch.

Of course, Pater, they have a wide gauge [referring to railroad trackage] system here, but in and around camp runs about a 30 inch gas locomotive and the same small 2 way dumps that were on the Isthmus. [Harris' father was involved in purchasing surplus equipment in Panama, following the termination of the French company contract for construction of the canal.] Damned, when I first saw them, I thot if I only had 'em over at the plant, they'd sell like hot cakes.

What else can I write? This must be interesting. I've got to make some arrangements with a bank to keep my finances.

| | |
|---|---|
| $280.00 | I brot over with me. |
| 10.00 | for tips on boat |
| 160.00 | last month's pay that I hope Bud is bringing over. |
| 176.00 | This month's pay—ten percent additional for overseas |
| $626.00 | |

On basis of 5.6 Francs per dollar: 5.6 x 626 = 3505.6 francs.

I've got to buy a few things such as trench coat, etc., yet so combining financial and clothing requirements mite suffice to furnish me with military mission to get somewhere. A truck train goes to place where Mann is every other day. I'll try to make it some day.

How are you all? Even at this early date I'd give 3505 of the above Francs to see you all, or even Buns, i.e., I'd give it out on interest of—say 15% per month. Of course, he had to spoil it! Such a sentimental thot.

I can see that my French will never be of much a/c. For a few weeks there, I got on pretty well, when we were "mushing" it alone, but now we never hear it. Of course, I remember such as: Fermez la bouche! Fermez la porte! Excuse spelling on a/c of the poor light.

I certainly hope you have all written long ere this. You know, any damned little thing—like Pater's kicking at the food, Marilee's bossing—Mater's mania for buying new stylish gowns and swell hats (no offense, Madam) all put the old wigor and wim back into one.

But one of my men was rite when he said, "Now don't worry about me (he was writing his first letter home after landing) I'll be all rite as long as I'm with Uncle Sam." No one would want for a thing. No Hooverizing at all—[Herbert Hoover was in charge of the United States Food Administration. To Hooverize meant to save food for civilians in Europe, especially in Belgium.] Y.M.C.A.'s doing wonderful work, etc. And they say the nearer one gets to the front the better everything gets as regards food, assortment and the like. So why worry? You even get sheets up in the officers' billets for a franc or 40 cents a day which includes cleaning your boots.

*With lots of love,*
*Harv*

P.S. Never felt better in my life!


*Sunday Afternoon*
*April 28, 1918*


DEAR MATER,

It's funny, but now I know I should be an artist or poet. I have planned on writing you day after day, but I have not "ze inspeeration," and the time does go fast. I really believe it has been a week since my last letter.

Of course the whole point is this: confined to this camp and with nothing exciting doing—it's no different than any camp. It's possible there's a war going in, and outside of the fact that we follow the *N.Y. Herald* or *Daily Mail* quite closely—the daily bulletin and the map—we mite just as well be back in the States. Hence I ask, "What can I write about?"

First—and very happily so—Rudy [Rudy Matthews, a college friend] is at this camp. He came in about Thursday. You know I wrote you that I'd heard he was coming back from school, and that I'd waited several nites for him around the Officers' Club. Well this nite I walked around the mess-room and there was this little "fire-eater." For about 15 minutes there the Colonel must have been a little peeved—at the greeting with him mostly on my part, and on the part of the other 6th battery men with our outfit. "Well, well, well, how are you? Where've you been? Trays beans!"

There are about eight of the 6th Battery men here now, and about 10 more expected next week. We're going to have a supper tonite at the French officers' club here in camp. It auto B a beaner with everyone of us trying to yell out our experiences at once—and the more so with Sauterne as cheap as Lithia water [mineral water with lithium salts.]

I've got to break in here and tell you what happened yesterday. Four of us, Rudy, Syk, and Lt. named Peters and myself went for a 2 hrs. ride over beautiful French roads and thru those old quaint French villages where the main streets look like alleys and smell like barnyards, evidently homes of the poorer peasants with ox teams, cows, etc., running around loose, but almost always you see a large church in a town of 400 or 500 people.

The ride was wonderful. The horses were all new remounts and tres frisky. Mine wouldn't let one of the other nags get within hearing distance. And it was pretty warm. I believe I worked harder than the nag.

At last we got to a little place about 5 or 6 miles from here, and it was so fine and cool riding thru that village the road protected from the heat by damp-looking stone buildings, covered with moss and centuries of dirt—that we decided to stop in the tavern and have ze drink of vin blanc. So we dismounted and went in. As cool as a cave. Heavy-hewn timbered ceiling, big fireplace—everything suggestive of great age. After we'd finished a bottle or two of sauterne, Ooh la la! Syk asked her how old the old place was. "Cent Cinquante." S'possible? Then we marvelled at the wonderful preservation of the place as students of art and wines are wont to do—and I starting to arise—caught me spurs in the peculiar seat contraptions and snapped off the seat. The other birds haven't got over kidding me yet. Hells, bells—it was only about ¼ inch stuff and rotten all the way thru. A 150 year old seat isn't hard to wreck.

Outside of the fact that on the way back Matty's saddle slipped around (and we were just going up a steep slope) I looked around and there was his horse bucking around with Matty rolling down the hill. Well, anyway, we got back for retreat.

This morning the enlisted men of the Ammunition Train HQs. played the officers a five inning game of ball. It was a lot of fun. I didn't play, as I developed several W. K. charley horses at early practice. Major Hunter, an old West Point ball player, was the star for a few innings. Then he "broke."

Is that new regulation in effect re sending packages over here? I have to send you a request O.K.'d by my captain and you are to put it in package you send. Don't send cigarettes. I can get more than I need. (For 3 months at least. I have that much now.) And the food we're getting is excellent. So honestly I'm absolutely sitting pretty! And I only hope you all are feeling as fit and as content. The biggest thing in this adventure is the camaraderie, and you'd have to go far to find a better bunch of men.

Well, Mater, it's 10 o'clock and I've been pounding around the Ecuries [stables] all day.

*My best love to all,*
*Harv*


*Monday Afternoon*
*April 30th, 1918*

DEAR PATER,
I got your letter mailed from New York on April 2, just this noon. That isn't so bad. It doesn't bother one much—(busy all day and tired at nite) until some bird gets some mail and even passes up mess to read them. Then you get to thinking, and I've just about come to conclusion that it doesn't do to think too much about—what would I be doing if at home now; how long will we lay around on this side. It's easy to get pretty low taking that kind of dope.

I believe the latest dope on service chevrons, i.e., stripes on the arm for every six months of service—is that all in France or England get them after that length of time. Oct. 1 will bring me my first.

We're not doing a thing exciting here, as I am attached to Horse sec-

tion. We are detailed temporarily on the remounts and with a large detail we just put in 8½ hrs. a day, "chamber-maiding."

More anon.

*Love to all,*
*Harv*

Request slip to be put in pkge.


*May 7, 1918*

Dear Folks,
I am O.D. [officer of the day] today and am taking my first opportunity
of sitting down and actually resting during the day-lite hours, since
I arrived at this camp. In some hard campaign some years ago the
officers of an outfit "reared" a little about the severity of the work.
A killing pace, etc., etc. The C.O. said, "But the nite is 12 hrs. long, isn't
it?" It were then, but not here. Reveille 5:30 A.M. Recall 6:10 P.M. and 2 or
3 hrs. of nite work.

So today, in addition to my work with the ponies, I am O.D. To my
sergeant at the stables I said, "You'll find me in my quarters." The same
to my O.G. (officer of the guard). The O.D. is also Police officer, in
charge of cleaning up, sanitation drainage, etc. To my provost sergeant
I also said the same. Damn it, I got to have some system, or all H will be
looking all over for me. There's only one drawback—the Colonel! He'll
probably claim that I don't cover enuf territory sitting down. "I will, sir,
shortly if this excellent mess of ours continues—if I don't now."

I still put in interesting days. Take yesterday for instance: stable
sergeant up to 5 P.M., battalion adjutant for retreat, O.D. rite after that.

I wrote I got Pater's letter from N. Y.; a note from Stadilman dated
April 10 (yesterday I got this) and plenty of advertising. If I had the say
I'd forbid the use of foreign mails to printed matter. Some bird tells
you there's a letter at Hqs. for you. You rush over and it's some announcement that Madame Bohunkus is opening a manicure shop on
Broadway, Sanitary and up to date! And for me, for whom manicurists
were always so undesirable.

I figure, tho, that you probably got my cable (about April 12 or 13th)
sent the day we arrived and that the next two or three days should
bring me a wad of mail.

I haven't been out of camp since I hit it—and further more don't see any opportunity in the near future at least. Yesterday and the nite B4 the officers had to patrol the wine rooms on the road just outside of camp. Why was that, Mr. Whitewash? Well, sir, our men received their first pay in 2 or 3 months Saturday nite, and with this severe schedule they were bound to go out on a tear. And some did get "liquered." One fellow picked up by the M. P.s cried continually, "I wanta to go home to Lieut. Vogel. I wanta go home to my Lieut." Another bud being roughly handled by the M.P.s (national guarders) yelled out, "Come on you regulars." It's a good thing none were around or this mite have been trouble.

My main dissipation has been to slip down to the French officers' mess nites with Rudy and other playmates and kill a couple of bottles of Sauterne. It's wonderful.

And say, do you sleep nites! So tired that when you turn in you feel like spreading out and just sort of flow all over the bed like a jelly—a little going over the edge of the cot. If you were ever dog tired U'll get my drift. Complete relaxing of every muscle!

Honestly, there isn't much to write! Went over to the officers' "Y" after dinner, sat around awhile until the paper came in and played the "Victor" [Victrola]. It certainly is fine.

Between Rudy, several others and myself, we expect to take over the whole Champagne sector by May 15th; and talking about war! There's a new fearsome thing that altho not a direct result of present war, nevertheless has been made more general than ever—and that's Cork shock. At first like shell shock it really worries you, but later there's no physical reaction, just pecuniary. That's a hot one!

Kiss Buns for me, and best love to all,

*Harv*

*Mother's Day.*

Dear Mater,

It is now about 10:30 P.M. and I just got back from a swell horse-back ride of about 3 hours—to the same place that I wrote you about a couple of weeks ago: when I snapt a bench in two, a bench which was 150 years old. Remember?

Rudy, Knox, Burno, Fossland, Beacom and Burns and myself. Swell party! I had a fine horse that could trot like a fiend and if you think it isn't exhilarating to speed thru this wonderful country on magnificent roads with good mounts and my "buddies," you miss your guess.

I just have to remark on the way a change of scene, a little wine and good companions can pep one up. Ever since I've been here including Sundays, I've been in the stables, and to say it gets worrisome is putting it mildly.

Well, when orders came this morning to feed water and even groom B4 quitting—and on Sunday too—I just got damned mean! I was that way all day; and then when it got to 5 P.M. this afternoon and still not finished—after I'd promised myself to write you sure today on Mother's Day—I certainly lost my sweet disposition. But now everything's sitting pretty!

Syk and the other Motor section officers just got back with some trucks from a debarkation point; and all were filled with enthusiasm over Normandy and its apple blossoms.

Do you remember the last day of Camp when you and Aunt Annie called for me and we picked up Stansbury at Highland Park? He's here, so is Armour—who drove our ambulance here a year or so ago—and who was in my battery. In fact about 30 6th Battery birds are here from school and we "hard" regulars are certainly making them realize how little they know. When I was O. D. a Lt. from my battery was officer of the guard. He said, "What in 'ell do U do, when, how?" What do I say, "You know I got 98 on my exam at Fort Sheridan on guard duty and haven't had time since, too busy at school here." I patted him fraternally on the shoulder, looked at my watch and said in a sweet voice, "You haven't had time—it's just 15 minutes to guard mount. C that U find time now." Honestly we're so hard we spit against the wind.

There isn't anything else of current events; and I could write a lot of how I feel on this day, set aside as Mother's Day—when I can figure just what you are doing and what you all are thinking of. But your thots are mine—and let's let it go at that!

So Babe has gone to Custer! Fine, and I'm damned glad he is so interested. The test, tho, is to keep it up. I know he will. Because one can certainly have "low" moments in this old war game—just as in anything else, and then it takes all you got to keep on going—just like after the first 5 minutes of a football game.

Love and Cheerio, good luck and only to say further that I am as comfortably situated here in all respects as any camp yet—so don't worry or imagine things.

Best regards to all the family,

*Harv*

*Sunday, May 19, 1918*
*Somewhere in France*

DEAR FOLKS,

Imagine a beautiful summer morning in May, the apple blossoms which have made Normandy famous, in bloom; and peace and quiet that one might find up on Lake Baraboo, and me just returning from my morning's tour of inspection of the stables on a swell horse! Could anything be sweeter? And furthermore not much more to do today as I saw to it yesterday that enough forage was issued to last until tomorrow.

You see until Saturday I was a common stable sergeant purveying to some 500 horses. I am now Supply Officer of the Remount Depot issuing feed etc. to many times 500, superintending, requisitioning supplies, etc.

The S.O. (supply officer, formerly) is now in charge of my section. He was assigned for specific purpose of S. O. at Chickamauga, but was rode pretty hard by the Major and Col. the last week or so—and I am now the guy. But I guess they must feel sorry for me or else disgusted, or perhaps I handle 'em rough and they like it. Nary a remark!

Thus instead of pounding my feet off from 7 until 5—I have my horse outside the door of Hqs. on a picket line, slip off every little while and generally lead a life befitting a veteran of 1 yr. and 9 days service.

The first thing Bud [Bud Fisher] told me about was the party Pater put him thru. He admitted he had weakened, in fact passed out, but that it was quite a stunt to last as long as he did. Incidentally he brot my check. I've got about 3500 francs and another pay day staring me in the face. Some day you'll get a check or N. Y. draft from me for some couple thousand. All kidding aside, I want Im and El [Imogene and Eleanor, sisters of Harris] to get about 50 bucks each and go down to Fields and buy any damn thing they want. And as for Buns—she can go the limit. It wouldn't be hard for me to eat my roast beef at the family board today, just entre nous. Our life here is damn nice. Take this afternoon for instance! We (Rudy, Syk, Bud, Fossland, Knox) are going out at about 2 bells, ride along, and eat supper somewhere-arriving back at 9 or 10. Not so bad, eh? Then we'll stop at the French officers' mess for Sauterne or Creme de menthe. I believe Sherman was too pessimistic. [Referring to the remark, "War is hell" of Civil War General Sherman.] Almost every nite after supper we go out for a couple of hours B4 dusk and, believe me, no matter how a guy feels, this ride perks him up.

Oh yes, I got a box of *Lozanos*, tres bon, from Pater. When were they sent? Perhaps that order doesn't pertain to officers because that box rode right thru—it was stamped at some N.Y.P.O. "content examined" and it must have been sent after April 1.

Knox, Rudy, Syk, Foss and I bum around quite a bit—in fact all the time, together. And there are some bunk sessions regarding all important events. You know the old hot-stove stuff. Well, since we've been in the army there has been enuf of it released to gas every Boche around.

I received a swell letter from Mater, dated the 6 April and thot the part about Babe's clothing not fitting very humorous. I haven't found any issue stuff that fits. The big thing in the army is neatness. The clothes don't have to fit just so there are a few places not spotted and a crease. You would be surprised how one's attention is attracted to a man with clean, pressed clothes. Often you can't place the man's face, but identify him by clean-cut appearance. I think it's great Babe takes an interest just finding himself.

We get the late dope every nite at the Y. where we can get the *N.Y. Herald, Daily Mail* and *Chicago Trib*. Right now awaiting news of the expected drive which the Boche fell down on 4 or 5 days ago.

Pater asks, "RU in action?" Hell, no. Won't be for some time.

Oo la la! Just got 9 (N*I*N*E) letters. And if you think it wasn't wonderful! I just read them once but will go over them again tonite. It takes a month to 5 weeks for a letter to reach me.

I am certainly glad that you, Mater cherie, don't worry about us. Become a fatalist. If you are going to get it you are just as likely to eat too many pancakes some morning and kick off, as stop a bullet. That must have been quite a sight the morning Mater and Im and Marilee ran downstairs in their undershirts when my postcard came. I suppose the little macher just stood at the table and ate in every word. I can see her standing there in her woolly pajamas with the feet about 7 inches too long.

Heard a good one the other day: An American in a German prison camp wrote, "Am getting wonderful treatment, the food is fine. Nothing to do. Wouldn't leave if I could. In fact the only place I'd rather be right now is Calvary."

That's the funniest thing I ever heard. Babe a cook. At last, Mater, he has a chance to make good. It isn't such a bad job if he can get to be mess sergeant. You know a cook in the army has more privileges than a C.O. Everybody humors him. Supposedly an artist with the usual temperament, he gets out of drilling and it's up to the C.O. to keep him in good spirits.

Babe writes, "I suppose I will rot away in this unit." Every guy in the army is the same in this respect—never satisfied—but always kicking.

Honestly, this thing is moving too fast, I start my letter with loud exclamations about being Supply officer for Remount Depot. By noon tomorrow I turn over that job. We are being relieved, i.e., the whole train, from this remount detail. Then I don't know what I'll be doing. Maybe we'll all get 24 hours leave. Yet, maybe not.

When I get a chance to leave this camp, possibly this week after relieved of the Remount, I'm going to pick up some trinkets and send them home. Maybe some Brittany lace made by the peasants.

Love and kisses

*from Harv*

P.S. The lil ole picture album is a great thing. Carry it always and when "low" once in a while, sit down on a bale of hay or a pile of manure and ruminate.


*May 28, 1918*


MA CHERIE,

I just wish you could take a squint into this room now. And I certainly hope the colonel doesn't! Two-thirty in the afternoon—Monday, too, with Rudy and Bud taking some bunk fatigue and me writing—to a large degree because there are only two beds. I suppose you all think "how awful—living in dirty dugouts—no conveniences—bitter cold and canned food." In reality I look out of my window now onto a beautiful stucco bungalow with showers and dressing rooms like the C.A.C. [Chicago Athletic Club]. Have the same food we would get in the States and considerable siestas.

Isn't it a coincidence that Rudy's quarters aren't more than 75 feet from mine? He has a corner room, quite exposed to passersby—so after he takes the battery out in the A.M., puts in charge 2 or 3 2nd Lts. (who take orders from him), then he returns here.

Bud is Asst. Adjutant with little to do except keep from being seen too much. I am Supply Officer. Just the other day I got that job. The first time I have been at any one place long enough to be assigned. As long as the Horse section is with Motor I'll have practically nothing to do—but when we go up and are separated my work will begin. I can't help but reiterate how I enjoy these different assignments with no chance to get into a rut, I may be kidding myself.

I am kind of tired myself this afternoon, having arrived back at 2 A.M. and standing reveille at 5:45 A.M. So unless one of these birds gets up shortly, I'll have to pull some of this latest stuff viz. R.H.I.P. (rank has its privileges) and rout one of them out. Having received our commissions on the same date lots were drawn for seniority. I drew #6 of first Lts. Bud's further down and Rudy's only a second Lt. The point is this—when all the Majors, Cpts. etc., stop some shells and also 5 Lieuts., I'll be in command. Great prospect, n'est-ce pas?

Now a few words about my trip. Friday noon I got a hunch to go with truck train that night to ____ where Mann is, and dammit I almost missed it because it was 5 o'clock before I woke up, and the train leaves at six P.M. I rushed up to the Major—"nicked" him hard [Gave a proper salute]—sort of stampeding like—told him I wanted to go on official business to buy some baseball equipment for Fossland's Company. The latter gave me permission. "Oui," parled the Colonel, so I got away quick. Capt. Hoyne aussi. Supper at 9:30, half way, and kidded some French girls—then left for destination—arriving there about 1 A.M.

Slept until 10 A.M. next morning, first time since I left the good old ship that I haven't stood that terrible reveille. Don't believe I'll ever get used to it. It's the only custom that worries me so that sometimes I wonder why I ever started to play this game. After an 8 or 10 egg omelet and Benedictine etc., we started bumming around. At about 10:45 my official business was finished. There were no baseball outfits here. At least that was what some guy told me. I couldn't be bothered to inquire.

I went over to see Mann at noon. His work doesn't appeal to me—too much like a Chicago river wharf gang. Non pour moi! I'm a fighting man—drink swamp water and spit against the wind. "Shure," says Aunt Annie. "Wonderful macher, doesn't know when he'd be well off." Well, I am satisfied to let those birds wear service chevrons, but I'd prefer the least desirable from a physical standpoint. I don't include Babe's outfit in that class because from the little I have heard the Hospital units get enough excitement and then some.

### 9 P.M. continued—

After supper to-nite Bud, Fossland and a couple of other Lts. and I played horse-shoes for a couple of hours, chewing tobacco etc.—just like Sunday on a farm back of the ole manure pile. Oh, it's a hard life.

I believe I wrote there appeared a camp order forbidding any horse-riding out of camp. C'est tres mal! [It's very bad.] Some crazy guys got plastered and galloped like mad. Well that's over now and I am looking forward to more evening riding on my "Garibaldi," a wonderful horse, [can] outrun, outwalk, outjump any horse in the stable.

*Lt. Harris riding Garibaldi during*
*his assignment to the Remount Services.*

Oh, yes, I forgot to write that we inadvertently missed the truck train last night to bring us back here. But you can't fool us—we are too smart. Just step up to Hqs., hand them our line, get a Dodge and hit it up at about 50 per, overtaking it in about an hour. I suppose the inhabitants of little villages thot it must have been Pershing [General John J. Pershing, commander of the American Expeditionary Force.] leaving to superintend a "big drive." After feed at 9 P.M. Capt. Hoyne and I crawled up on a truck of oats, got under a heavy tarpaulin and had a four hour sleep under a wonderful moon. Could anything be sweeter? Met the motor section on the way—going to—get oats.

From all indications we will remain ici for a couple of months. I suppose that's when the band quits playing and the kickoff starts the biggest game yet. Lots of love,

*Harv*

*Friday, May 31, 1918*

MA CHERIE,

No inspiration tonite—but it's 10 o'clock and I am not a bit tired, except of chewing the rag; first with Rudy, then in Bud's room and last Fossland's [from Winthrop Harbor, Illinois]. Just as most of our enlisted men start their letters home, I say, "As I haven't any thing else to do I thot I'd drop you a line."

I think Pater's idea of sending carbons of my letters to different people a wonderful one because just to think that one of the originals should get lost and no copies made! An irreparable loss to the world's literature! You can censor them and send copies not only to the family, but to some of my former playmates.

One of the outfits that reached here a week ago has been doing the M.P. work at this camp. They are going away. So we take it over in the next day or so. At officers' meeting this morning the colonel cautioned the company commanders to put their best men on this work—because on the appearance, efficiency, and bearing of this guard—will we be judged. Hence in keeping with this statement he detailed me as officer in charge which, of course, was the only proper and fitting course to take. So beginning Monday I will get the finishing touches to my otherwise hard career. I should say to my hardening process for after handling "stews, fites" at all hours and other forbidden liaisons I should be ready to fight anyone. Besides, altho Garibaldi is a gentle riding animal, beating the seat of a motorcycle side car all day will be a suitable help to this process.

There are and will be a lot of things in my letters to you alone—because no doubt I do get clubby often. Frinstance I keep telling you I'm "good"—all to the "Jake," so to speak. There is no use talking about it. I heard thru channels a few days ago something that perked me up. You, no doubt, have heard of qualification cards that are filled out for every enlisted man, listing his previous experience under some 200 to 300 headings. WELL we made out one for ourselves. It is graded by one's superior officer.

| | | | |
|---|---|---|---|
| 15% | – Military bearing | | |
| 15% | – Physical qualities | | |
| 15% | – Mental qualities | on this basis | |
| 15% | – Forget this one | 100%—is perfect | |
| 40% | – Value to service | | |

I got 95—very likely fell down on the "mental." Incidentally it was the highest grade in the train including Majors and Captains. Some were very low. So I'm not sitting so bad with my major, who graded mine. This is one of those points mentioned above.


## Continued, June 5, 1918

Last Saturday afternoon I went to _____ about 30 miles from here with the officer I am relieving. Our purpose was to go over the town which I imagine to be about the size of Madison, Wisconsin, and to have pointed out to me the various lures the men are likely to get hooked in. U C every Saturday a certain % of this camp get passes for that place. None given during the week. Hence the necessity of having M.P.s there for their protection. So every Sat. I have to hike there and either stay over till the men return Sunday nite or else return & go back Sunday. It's a beautiful ride and I can make it in an hour.

It was the most peculiar experience I have ever had. To go into these gilded palaces, be introduced as the new M.P. officer, with a "hard look" discuss the points with the proprietor (male or female) that may give trouble; in other words act like a Chicago police captain. All the places are licensed and regulated by the French gov't. The only control we have over them is to forbid them to our men if necessary and prevent any trouble.

The above comparison with the Chicago Police is more true than I first thot because they all work the old game. Try you out by offering their best vintage. Suffice to say, that, altho I was wont to go and have my Epernay or Sauterne regularly, they are off my ration card from now on—or until I am relieved of this assignment. I figure that's the only way to "get by."

I really report to no one, have no set rules to go by. Results count. Go anywhere I want at any time—within reason, of course. In other words, I'm on my own as never before since being in the army. I'm standing formations as best as I can and as often, so I don't get too much "out of it." It looks as tho we are going up in a couple of weeks and fight the w. k. Northern mud. Hence it won't pay to miss any special instructions that may arise.

The first thing in the A.M. I receive reports from my non-coms in charge of details. Then report to Hqs. (as I have practically no connection with Ammunition Train—my order reading "detailed under Camp commander") and put in my charges: Some men out after taps, drunk, disorderly constitute main charges. Then I ride around, on and off, until 4 P.M. when I have a formation and inspection of my M.P.s, both the dismounted and mounted men. At 7 P.M. I make the rounds again because that's the most trying time. Outfits are being paid and when there is money there's liquor and fites. My beat is about 35 miles i.e., a radius of 5 miles or more around camp.

June 17 is your anniversary, Mater and Pater. We may be very busy about then and I mite not get time to write or cable, but being over here gives a man plenty of food if not time for thot. To write my thots on this happy occasion would make them seem to me—not exactly bromidic but failing entirely to convey my thots. Use mental telepathy and what you think is what I mite write.

Lots of love and happy wishes. Trays beans.

# 3

# TANKS
# ARE FOR ME

**TANK CORPS**

**TREAT EM' ROUGH**

*A.P.O. #714*
*Somewhere else in France (Langres)*
*June 13, 1918*

MA CHERIE,

They say it's all in the way you "step it off," and I don't know how to start this letter except by saying that I'm now a Tanker. You all probably have thot I was B4 on c/o my numerous trips to Al's and Jim's, but this is the first time I have been officially recognized as such. You don't get me? Well, since yesterday I'm an officer in the 301st Tank Center, and unless I get kicked out for something, will probably get what I've always secretly wanted, viz, in perfect safety to playfully swing a machine gun back and forth at a row of advancing Boche, and see them go down like trees in a big wind. That's accomplishing something! Then there is another minor point. It's practically a new corps. Men R enlisting in the States for this service, so about Thanksgiving I can see myself just as plain as anything, manouevering one at Grant Park with office at LaSalle St. somewhere—sent back for instruction purposes. Just wait and see! With Buns riding up in the turret and a good old Thanksgiving dinner waiting. Merveilleux! [Marvelous.]

It happened in this way: About the 1st of the month a bulletin came out from Gen'l Hqs. calling for men and officers to apply for the Tanks. Only about 11 officers from our outfit applied including a major, Knox Burns, Bud, Syk, myself and others. Then with customary army pow-wows we waited for the answer. Mine came first, last Saturday. It looked bad to have to leave my buddies & go alone. Then Sunday Lt. Longstrethe's came, and Monday, Bud's. Monday night we took a Ford for Rennes (A late order allows us to mention towns in the base sections so I can tell you we were at Coetquidon near Guer, about 60 miles from St. Nazaire) and took a night train for Paris.

So this is Paris! Altho in a 1st class compartment we had no berths so we curled up the best we could, but it was damned cold. I had all my stuff packed up, of course, where I couldn't get it, and had only a raincoat to cover myself with, but Hell's bells what's that with Paris only a few hours away!

After disposing of as much baggage as ever arrived on any one train for only 3 officers, we got a taxi and went to the American University Union. You know what that is? Kept up and sponsored by American

*Recruiting poster for the Tank Corps, with its "Treat 'Em Rough" motto.*
*Poster designed by August William Hutaf.*
From the copy in the Rare Book Collection, University of North Carolina.

Universities. And funny thing,—the first one I ran into was Rick Matthews. [College friend] He just finished his flying training and was taking 3 days leave to go down and see Rudy. He had breakfast with us and caught a 7:30 train.

Then I started down along old familiar haunts but O mores! O Passing Years! Of course I recognized the Place de l'Opera, with the Grand Hotel on one corner and the *Daily News* office across the street. And the Madeleine! And I figured on making the Margary Cafe, as I remembered it straight down from the Grand Hotel, but never got there. And that was all.

We walked a lot and rode some down the Bois de Bologne, Champs Elysees etc., but it was just like hitting a place for the first time. It was some place tho, I'll tell the world.

We had dinner at the Officers Y.M.C.A. presided over by, I believe, a Mrs. Roosevelt [Mrs. Theodore Roosevelt, Jr., daughter-in-law of former President Theodore Roosevelt] and it was pretty nice to see a good old American girl again. I don't want to become rheumatic or sedimental—but there's a difference, especially living as we were practically isolated for 3 months.

At about 3 P.M. we sat at a table out in front of Cafe de la Paix—you know, just accidentally found it like and watched 'em go by. If anyone says the French are nervous or worried with the enemy a 10 minute aeroplane ride away—just let him see the thing as we did. In the first place our yellow cab drivers couldn't take in enuf to keep a bird alive in competition with the French. They run wild, take corners at 40 mi.—yet never an accident. The streets are crowded with civilians and every kind of soldier and as far as the women,—well if I were a betting man, I'd wager that with 100 cards to play, the last would be the best. And a sure win on every card. Of course, I'm only looking at it from a paregorical, that is to say, aesthetic standpoint. From all other angles the cards are stacked, surer 'n 'ell!

Longstrethe met a 2nd Lt. who is Black Jack's [General John J. Pershing] Aide. Rides all over with him. Just came in with him from somewhere. We all had supper at the Cafe de Paris. Then to the Casino de Paris—like the Folies Bergere only more so. In fact, I never saw anything like it—but there's still more work to be done here so we moved out into the night.

No one thinks of air raids, taxis meet you as usual and all in all there's less outward thot put on the war than we'd put on a Boston Store Clearing Sale.

I was very sorry not to have met anyone I knew from Chicago, but pertate [perhaps] apres la guerre [after the war]. Will make another letter out of it.

Love,

*Harv*

*June 15, 1918*

You can see then that there was nothing special about our day's stay in Paris. We had to get down to the station very early to find our baggage—which we had to check there—then hire a fleet of three taxis to transport it to another station—14 pieces averaging the size of a locker. Remember that big bag you sent me from Fields? It must have weighed forty pounds alone. All along the line the baggage men would say "Boku Baggage." [Beaucoup—a lot of.] And before we got thru with it, it cost us boku francs. Most of the officers have lost or stored theirs at some Q.M. Bud and I are going to have an auction. It's a cinch I'll not move from here with any of it. Up in the lines one is allowed 30 pounds total. That means bedding roll and a pair of shoes.

I don't know how long this training lasts, probably a month or so. It will be great work and very instructive. The hours are not long. U R really on your own to learn the different machine guns, technique, etc., and pass the courses as quick as you can.

Now let me go back and pick up a few odds and ends. I wrote you I was detailed as military police officer for Coetquidon. Had the job for about a week and it was swell. Most interesting and you could get as much excitement as U wanted. During the day there wasn't much to do. Just bunk fatigue and time to "wonder why." Go out in my side-car for a while—most of the time I could be found in my quarters. It was fine. My Major made it a point to walk by my room pretty often, until finally I pinned some newspapers over the windows—just to keep out the glaring light.

The more you'd move around at night the more you run into fights, drunks, etc. Every once in a while some bird gets arguous and you are compelled to crown him—make him a king in other words. I carried a loaded quirt but only had to use it once.

One night my M.P.s beat up a drunken artilleryman, and when I got there at about 9 P.M. the fellow's entire battery was there to clean us up. I put out a skirmish line & rounded them up. They said they were looking for him. "All right, go back and come back with a commissioned officer and you can look all you want." They did. This was about 10 P.M.—moonlite and blowing and crispy, sort of hazy, on an elevated plateau. Pay strict attention to this setting. While waiting for anything to happen, I looked around and saw a little kid, hands in pockets and teeth chattering and very dejected-looking. "Allez couches," [Go to bed] I said. He moved off and I noticed he was crying. A Frenchman started talking to him and I could gather from the conversation that this little kid was a refugee from Valenciennes—northern France—that he had been walking for a month sleeping and eating anywhere—and with not a soul in the world, his parents and folks killed. I sent him up to my quarters after giving him four eggs and an immense sandwich. How he got here I don't know. Nothing else happened in my tour so when I got back Syk had fixed him up with a bed and he was sitting pretty.

The story of my "petit" got all over the regiment next morning and there was much excitement. Several YMCA men wanted the story for the village gazette. Others were for taking up a fund. Petit was mostly interested in the question of whether he could stay with us forever. When we said "yes," he beamed. Bud brot him a khaki suit, underwear, O.D. shirt, socks etc. and all fitted him pretty well. He was happy as a lark and saluted every one. Then our striker gave him a bath, but to do so our striker had to go under first. He liked it so much he wanted another that afternoon. Unfortunately I was leaving, myself, that afternoon. I sure would have liked to take him along. Just before I left I was sitting in Knox's room and he walked by, crying. I went out and called him, but he continued on to my quarters and when I got there, he said "vous allez?" He saw my baggage all rolled up. "Oui, retournez toute suite." Then he smiled but I knew darned well I would never see him again. I reported him to my company commander and he will probably be turned over to some society. Had I time to remain I might have been able to work out something for him. Maybe some of the other fellows will look out for him.

Knox and Syk put in for the tank corps and I certainly hope they get here. Will know in the next few days. There was quite a farewell when we pulled out, from the colonel down. You can imagine—playing together for almost six months every day, organizing the train and fighting the war from every angle. But you can't close shop on that account. The colonel said he was sorry to see us go and would have a hard time replacing us, but realized it was a more interesting branch, and one where we could do more service, which all of us concurred in—or would never have put in an application for it. Major of my battalion wrote in my personal history book, "An excellent officer in every respect." And if my other buddies get here I'll be sitting pretty. They expect 18 additional officers in the next day or so. They might be in the bunch.

This work besides being tremendously interesting and active is comparatively safe. Hell, we go out in an armoured car, along with and usually in the rear of the doughboys. So you can see how safe it is. Further there is no dugout life—but we live back in billets in fair comfort. Oh, I imagine it's fine. Even the fellows who are in it think it is the "nuts." So just sit tight.

*Harve*

My address
301st Tank Center
Amer. E. F.
A.P.O. 714
Via New York

*June 18, 1918*

It's a funny thing, but I've lost all ideas of seasons or periods. Except when I read in Pater's letters of his contemplated fishing trip did I remember that it was spring. In other words one's whole viewpoint changes. In civil life you can look up to certain things—fishing on Decoration Day, swimming at the beach in July and August, White Sox ball games, football seasons or buying a straw hat, but in the army, they are just 2 phases and no seasons. One you're in the trenches or two you're in training. Be it January or November . . . .

*311th Tank Center*
*June 30, 1918*
*In France*

DEAR ONES,

That "In France" always struck me as an impossibility when I was in the States. Something like a battle cry or call of the wild, but now, even in as short a time as three months it seems not at all strange. Why the noise of an elevated train or the like would work hard on me! I've always been out in the country where little girls chase cows with the help of a dog or two—where like clockwork they go out at 6 A.M. and return at 9 or 10 P.M. With their "allezs" and how they do yell! It just flows out. In the States it would take a teamster, no—a tempermental and disgusted music teacher would be more like it. We might say "get-to hell back on that road." They put at least three verses into it. What started me on all this? Oh, yes, that w.k. little girl just passed by with her herd. The French are certainly wonderful people. I can't imagine Americans accepting foreigners the way the French do. Take this instance—I was just returning from town and saw a buck private carrying a couple of large baskets, walking with an old grandmother, a mother and three petits. Evidently going out to spend the day in the country. It's this spirit! It's different with officers,—the only people we get to see are the peasants and the small tradespeople, and not the upper classes, and it's bred in the former people that officers are of the aristocracy. A Sam Browne belt [A leather belt with a diagonal shoulder strap to support a holster, worn primarily by officers.] will break up a family gathering. It's a cinch that whatever results of friendship do come about apres la guerre they will be done by the men and not the officers. They are the ones who are getting to the hearts of the people. They can't understand our happy-go-lucky spirit, tho. This war is a business to them—to our men it's a great sport—hard to reconcile the two.

And it seems as tho the men realize, at the same time, what they are here for—and are real soldiers. They are getting real discipline and appreciate its importance and also what they are here for. I've been to three or four camps always near towns of some size, and have noticed very little drunkenness, rowdyism, etc. Why, it's the greatest thing that could happen to them. Imagine the difference when they get back!

Most are from villages; a lot with no training of any kind except billiard hall or bar and then to get this broadening education! Merveilleux!

How do I get that way? Handing out this line in such an abrupt manner? Well I'll tell you. This is the most perfect day I have seen in a long while. Just like a June day in the North woods—a turn in the river—no bugs or mosquitos—anticipating a big Sunday meal and nothing to do until tomorrow. If Bud were here he'd say it was the glass of beer I had in town.

I wrote you that I was anxiously waiting for Knox and Syk to get here and that I received a wire from Knox. Thursday, in response to my letters, Major Whiting came over to see me. I was O.D. [Officer of the Day] at the tank center so he called on Col. Patton. The dope is that there are enough officers here now. So they are out of luck. Perhaps in time they'll get here, but by that time I will have moved on, so our sessions are likely over—until "Finis la Guerre." That's what makes it hard in this man's army—combinations always getting broken up. It comes down to playing alone as far as any permanent buddies are concerned. I have a hunch, too, that because of size, Bud may get with small ones and I with large ones. But give it to me, boy, it's the pick of the service. Plenty of excitement, and safe! Why "just as safe as a baby playing with a loaded revolver," as Pa Crowe [an English teacher at University High School] said on one of my themes. Remember? But jokes aside—when you go right along with the doughboys to clean out some nests of resistance and all you notice if the Boche hits you is a patter on the steel plate. Ain't it a glorious feeling!—with you pumping at them or moving right over and crushing their shelter.

There is a rumor afloat that a bunch of officers are going back to the States for instruction purposes. In the next week or so. Not for me! I'll do the trick about November. I didn't come over for a vacation with all expenses paid—to go back without a couple of "ears." I am getting too much raw meat. It's making me wild.

I got a *Daily Tribune* this A.M. dated April 23, but it was just as good as a late one. Read every word. I haven't had any mail for a couple of weeks. Suppose it will all come in a bunch. I imagine the Ammunition Train has moved up by this time. Nothing new. Taking reconnaissance work, now.

*Love,*
*Harve*

*June 21, 1918*

Mr. Frank Harris,
    Harris Brothers Company,
        Chicago, Ill.

DEAR MR. HARRIS:

I was very much pleased to receive your letter with Harvey's address but I am much more pleased to say that I have seen him.

Several days ago I was up town to see a fellow who was in the Engineers with me and as he and I came out on the street I noticed two officers standing nearby. Naturally I was real busy preparing to render a real soldierly salute when one of the officers turned toward me and I recognised Harvey. Well instead of proving myself a good soldier I hollered "Hello, Harvey." I guess it rather knocked him a little groggy for it is quite unusual for a soldier to address an officer by his Christian name. He didn't know me at first.

But what I want to tell you, F. H., is this. Since I have been in this man's Army I never have seen an officer that looked as good as Harvey. Now there is nothing or rather no one any more critical than a soldier when it comes to size up a superior. We all take orders without a word back but there are some officers that could lead a bunch of men thru H - - and never be obliged to utter a word. This may strike you as a rather secondary qualification, but as a matter of fact it is the essential element which enters into the successful career of the efficient officer. Such an officer is Lieut. H. L. Harris.

*Very Truly Yours,*
*/s/ George Cushman*


*311th Tank Center*
*July 14, 1918*

DEAR ONES,

Oo-la, la! Eight letters—count 'em—from Pater, Mater, Babe and Walt Lyon, dated all the way from April 21 to June 4 (just a month). I was getting just a little low as it was two weeks since I had the last batch—walking into the mess hall more and more often every day to see if there was anything for me and coming away lower than ever. We are living pretty confined here (taking this course of instruction) and this further tends to make us peevish. When Lo! the mail came. It didn't take me more than three minutes to read all the letters—and O! just like walking on air. I sat down to write this at once—But I had a chance to go to town in a machine last night and I took it. But I take this up later.

The thing of most interest was the celebration of the 4th in town. You probably read that today was also proclaimed a French Holiday and there was big doings everywhere and especially where American troops are located. In Paris, frinstance, there was a big track meet, a boxing contest, vaudeville, etc., at all of which big military and civil authorities were in attendance. I am sending you a copy of the *Tribune* in which U can note not only the programme, but also the general news we get daily. Besides that we have the *N.Y. Herald* and *Daily Mail*.

Be that as it may, I went to town last nite and after filling out a form (required by every lodging house) showing where born, date, etc., we got a room. Except for Paris I don't believe there are any bathtubs in France—no modern plumbing. I guess with all the street havens they don't need them. But the beds are wonderful. None of those flimsy iron things we have in second grade hotels made out of one-fourth inch tubing with the pink or yellow paint scaling off—but heavy all wood walnut, something like ours at home. The bedding included a 3 or 4 inch old style comforter. You can't fall into bed. You've got to jump in. Wonderful! It doesn't matter that there is no running water, or that you get a candle from the concierge who, unlike peacetime, is now usually an old lady, to find your way upstairs. None of that matters. You do sleep. And talking about candles we use them here most of the time whenever we want light. And to think that only three months ago I was playing around N.Y.

Everything closes up at 9 P.M. and we started out to walk just about that time. I felt as though I were back in 1600 A.D. The women outside closing the shutters, the people passing by talking a foreign language, the narrow cobblestone streets, and then a quiet neighborhood—two or three poilus [French soldiers] somewhat plastered, swaying arm in arm, from one curb to another singing the Marseillaise or maybe a rough song—loud as possible. Imagine it yourself and combine it with the feeling that you are over here to fight. But, of course, even the most romantic weaken. So after this pleasant experience of walking nowhere in particular with your thots thousands of miles away, Bud and I blew into the hotel and ordered up a flask of Sauterne to our room and proceeded to brighten up which we did satisfactorily. And, say, if prohibition goes into effect in the States before we get back there'll be Hell to pay. It will be easy to put it across with a million of us here fighting to make the world "Free for Democracy." Dirty pool—using the war to get us out of the way. Them's my sediments. It's all right in its place and we've got lots of place to put it. Proved the proposition right there. Voila!

This A.M. we got up late about 9:30, with a very cloudy taste and went out to look for breakfast but the law forbids service except at certain hours. We thot we might get a breakfast americaine at the Y but it was closed so we came back—had an omelette and chocolate and B and B for 1 franc 50 centimes (30 cents) at hotel. Very inexpensive—and we remark on that continually—how reasonable food is here—in fact, everything is cheaper here than in the States, equipment, clothing, etc. There was absolutely no need to bring over a million dollars worth of stuff. Can get everything here. Sometimes they are pretty strict if you don't have bread cards. We always promise we will bring some tomorrow. That's all they want so the authorities won't raise hell with them.

Speaking of the Tank corps—we were eating there this noon. Two very joli mademoiselles were sitting at another table avec American officers. Both fairly well lit up. One noticed our tank insignia (a tank we wear on our collar, same as the crossed-cannons of the Artillery) and pointing to other fille said, "Tanker, vous êtes tankers, n'est-ce pas?" "Oui, Oui, Oui, Oui!" and our French ran out.

Feel all choked up this Morning (6:30 A.M.). Tell U.Y. Mess is served from 6 to 6:30. Of course, we don't get up and start dressing before 6:18. Got it figured out to the second. 6 minutes to dress and 8 minutes to eat. It would be similar to suicide to walk in a minute late and have the colonel lamp you. Anyway their ideas of breakfast and mine are miles apart. Here is a week's breakfast menu:

> Monday   –  3 pancakes, coffee (no bread)
> Tuesday   –  2 small pieces of ham, coffee, 2 pieces toast
> Wednesday   –  see Monday
> Thursday   –  see Tuesday
> Sunday   –  2 eggs, coffee, 2 pieces of toast, big event

This morning I only allowed myself 3 minutes to eat.

Oh! that Charley Horse is nothing. It comes and goes with the damp weather. And re. silk underwear—What can I do with it? I sent all my laundry out one day and never got it back and I am glad of it. One suit of issue stuff is sufficient. When it's worn out or dirty, throw it away and have another suit issued. We get anything issued to us, just as enlisted men. That accounts for the fact that officers coming back from the front line bring only bedding roll, one pair of shoes and cigarettes—all they own. The more I can lose in driblets the less I'll have to throw away when I leave here. We are only allowed thirty pounds up in the line. I'll store my 385 pounds, but I never expect to see it again.

Pater wants to know if any of your letters have been censored. No—not so far. I don't believe I can get *Preferencias* or other cigars here, that's if I haven't sent you any requests. I have received 80 to 100 letters so far. That jibes with your estimate. They come in bunches of eight and ten.

Mater was wrong about my being in active service. Won't be for 2 to 6 weeks. I might just as well say "from one day to 2 months." Lots of rumors. I forget whether it is real rumors or ones that I have started. Lots of fun and gets a lot of worriers excited.

Cheerio, good luck and lots of love,

*Harve*

A.P.O. #714
*311 Tank Center*
*July 11, 1918*

There is nothing to write about work here at present—"carrying on" is about all. Knox, Syk (Colonel not Major any more) got their orders and I suppose have reported by now. Will give you the dope as soon as I hear from them. I understand they are moving within a mile of us. That would be nifty n'est-ce pas? And, say, aren't those birds sitting pretty! Hunter will be in command of quite an outfit. And to think that at one time he asked me to be his adjutant and I let him know in no uncertain terms what a rotten job I thot it was. He agreed with me. Knox told him in stronger words.

And along comes Syk who gets the job and I heard the other day—a captaincy. I understand that the three of us were up for it. Maj. Hunter said he didn't want to take us two because of our better faculty for handling troops. He preferred not to put us at a desk. And I hope it's so that Syk got his captaincy. He's a fine Boy. It's just one of those things that happen. "C'est la Guerre" as we say over here. Had we known what changes were to come about, viz. namely our transferring, we would have acted differently. Here is the point ("Yes, yes," says Pater). When one transfers it is without loss of rank. Get the captaincy, then transfer. But it was coming just as sure as shooting had we remained with the outfit. Ranking up high in outfit, highest mark on qualification, cards, etc., etc. And yet with all this I say, "Tanks for me and c'est la guerre. The war, it's the army, it's life." In other words this means, as the exclamation you have often heard when some poor misfortunate gets more misfortune, you say—It's life. Here we blame everything on the war—getting up for reveille, going out at night when it's raining like hell to watch a practice manoeuvre. C'est la guerre, and don't kick or crab.

But at the same time, mind ye, I see a situation. I worked on Lawrence for Knox and Syk. They work on Hunter pour moi; and I am just cocky enough now (smoking a *Lozano* from the box of 50 that Pater sent) to say that they won't have to work hard, either. But I know them. I'll bet they are on it now. "Leave him alone, nurse, he has only got cork shock and doesn't want to get well." One has to keep his mind active by assuming situations and then figuring out where they'll fall down. I can see Mater "wondering why." Don't do it, Mater.

*July 12, 1918*

DEAR MATER,

I just got 5 letters. Boku [Beaucoup] joli! I hasten to answer (because there surely can't be anything new since yesterday) where and how, oh how, did you get the idea that I was out of sorts. Sweet essence of Sauterne! Why I was figuring I was having the time of my life—and then to have Mater say that "reading between the lines" she gathered that I was, etc, etc. But honestly what do you refer to? When I write a couple of pages like this twice a week there isn't a thing I leave out—so if you read anything in you must be changing the sense Q.E.D. I am putting in a lot of detail—what I think—what he said—what she replied—otherwise there wouldn't be much to write. Summing up, while with the Ammunition Train, I always felt I was sitting pretty—if any guy was.

In first place I had the pick of 3,000 nags for riding purposes for myself. All I did was ride around and supervise the work like a southern landed proprietor riding over his estate. When I got bored I hiked out over the country, independent as a general. And never even got called. The Major of my battalion was wont to pick out one officer after another and "ride" them—we believed—just to see how they squirmed. Well, he got some so nuts they didn't know whether they were officers or not. I handled him "rough," told him what I thot about the discipline, etc., left my window open (in my quarters) so he could see me doing bunk fatigue at 10 A.M., as he invariably passed by— just got his number. He was the one who graded my qualification card, incidentally.

Well, with leaves off we have taken up a new diversion—looking at rectangular paste boards with numbers on them. The man who gets two with the same number wins. This reminds me of an English correspondent who visited an Australian camp over here and was explaining their games. One struck him as very odd, don't you know, and as Englishmen will, he explained, "They throw coins in the air to see if they will land alike or different."

Another German drive started yesterday and up to last nite they had not gained a single objective—perhaps feeling for a weak point. I don't know when we will get up. Nothing immediate, that's sure. It's a rotten feeling, tho, to be only 3 hours away—and dammit—and almost as far for the good you are doing—as in the U. S.

But when we do! WOW! This is a wonderful branch, and I consider myself lucky, coming over with the idea of transferring and to get this branch first crack. When you hit about five miles per hour over undulating country it's like sailing, and when you climb up the edge of a shell hole until perpendicular and you are sure you are going over backwards and then come down gently. Oh Boy it's a grand feeling! Wait until we get a little lore and tradition and more is known—we'll be using aviators for mechanics.

Right now I am instructing in elementary driving and you auto hear my line. It's nothing to talk for a couple of hours on attack, etc. So don't get the idea that all the Joes who return to the States and dwell in detail at suffragette meetings on "Your boy over there" ever saw action over here. You can pick up a lot over a bottle. Ask Harve, he knows.

*Beaucoup embrasses,*
*Harv*

*A.P.O #714*
*July 18, 1918—Sunday*
*311th Tank Center*

MA CHERIE,

I was meditating this morning walking out from _____ (5 miles from here) "wouldn't it be fine to get some mail and have all afternoon to answer it!" And sure enough—beaucoup—from Mater, Pater, Aunt Annie, Aunt Lettie and one from Jeannette Benjamin [another relative]. One from Pater was dated June 28th. Very good time, n'est-ce pas? I have noticed a lot that there has been a lot of investigation on somebody's part in reference to mail delay to soldiers. Maybe it has met with good results. Letters from home mean as much to a soldier as his mess. From the way we rush through a meal, for instance, when we have unread mail leads me to believe that if actual statistics were kept by sergeants of the mess—considerable savings are made on mail day, and that same has an actual food value.

There is a ball game going on between officers and men. An old captain who played with the Sox quite awhile ago is umpiring, and his characteristic announcement of batteries "for today's game" started some "what'd you be doing at home today in July on a Sunday afternoon avec *Lozano*?" Some Joe from Portland tells his idea, then a Southerner with hookworm "carries on." With the inevitable result an argument between everybody on East vs. West and South vs. North. Whether or not the North in '65 did not import Germans to fight the South, it's a knockout. Just across the walk from us is a hut inhabited by our Y.M.C.A. representative, our camouflager and other tankers. Always a poker game going on there, stud betting as high as a couple hundred francs on a card. They have a sign on their door "Buttercups Home." We're going to call this house the "Madhouse or the Padded Cell" or "Better Still," and believe me because of the continued argument it would be better, better still. Two medicos assigned to this outfit are bunking here temporarily. When they arrived Bud told them not to mind us because we're segregated on account of cork shock. One is an old Captain named Webb from Beaver Dam, Wisconsin. He reminds me of an old fashioned country doctor. They've been over less than a month. He drawls out "anything we can do for them?" "Yes," one inmate yells, "crown 'em all and make 'em kings." To crown from early English means to tap with an angular metallic substance thereby affecting the frontal lobe bringing on lack of consciousness and sometimes death.

The bunch of tankers here are fast building up great traditions and lore for this branch. They remind me of the Foreign Legion. Of course they haven't seen any fighting yet, but if they are as good at it as they are at killing, warming a deck, and being generally felt wherever they go, they'll be wonders. They have so intensely taken possession of several hotels that they are now dictating the policies thereof. No others are allowed in them. They have come from all branches of the service. Every one has his reasons for transferring—"hate to be in the S.O.S," "I didn't like our mess," "I wanted a trip through Paris." But for all— the lure of the Tanks.

This W.K. Southerner was with a negro regiment loading and unloading beef way back somewhere. He admits his outfit put up a service flag for him when he left, joking, "We all say that whenever a guy leaves a S.O.S. service it is customary to put up a service flag for him." This bird is worrying his life away for fear he'll be sent back. The only time he gets jovial is when "lit" then he keeps saying "good by Quartermaster corps!" The first night here he yelled out in his sleep "Bring on your Croix De Guerres, you (profanity)."

I am instructing in tank driving now, Bud in machine gun and "B" Longstrethe with me in driving. I like to just be around those darn little things, just like around horses. Certainly is fascinating. Especially when you always have a subconscious knowledge of what they can do, their potentiality.

I wrote you quite a while ago that Rudy's intended Father-in-Law was located here. A captain in Red Cross. I looked him up several times, but he was never in. He came down to see me yesterday. He is an official, I believe, in N. W. Mutual Life at Milwaukee. I took him for a ride in a Tank. He was intensely interested, never had seen one before. Very few over here. Our work, needless to say is not common knowledge, but Oh boy, wait until the "big thing" begins. It amused us to read the American slogan in the States, "We treat 'em rough."

The best thing he did (Palmer) was to give me a bunch of magazines. We read every word, mostly romantic stories, *Vogue*, and the like, and kept up to the times in re. latest colored shoes, new designs of chemise, etc. When any of the joes from any other hut wanted to read any of them I made them sign a memorandum receipt.

I received a cable from home three or four days ago, sent May 24th. About a month and a half to reach me. Longer than a letter. It came to me from England—but I believe that with the new E.M.F. service which I wrote you about in last letter by which cables are sent to Paris, service will be much quicker.

As a general thing on what day do you receive mail from me? Any special day? I suppose you get two or three at a time like I do, and yet your letters only mention receiving "a letter." Over here a little over three months, and have written you 20 letters almost two a week, not bad.

I see that you are getting rumors about Babe's outfit moving. It's the old stuff. Every outfit (has rumors) and everybody lives on them. It's so here, now, that whenever any Jake comes in and says "Shush" we all gather close, close all doors and windows—like a movie of a villain and his co-workers. The other day one came in "shushing" and after we all got quiet he said "We're going to have beans for supper." He was killed on the spot.

Mater, re a certain lieutenant taking a bath when his men were waiting for his signature on passes. Maybe the company clerk was told to take the passes down to him to sign. In other words, circumstances alter cases. That would never happen over here because we don't take baths. But you'll meet "low lives" in any endeavor. For everyone like the one you mention there are 1000 who'd pass up an invitation to dinner at a swell hotel with all the concomitants to go back to orderly room and see that all his men have proper clothing or look into what kind of mess they're getting. It's damned unfortunate to be in an outfit with an officer who is of the former kind. Maybe he'll learn. If he doesn't he'll "break" himself. But whether or not, remember always his rank. A phrase such as "knifing" in a private's letter such as was in yours, Mater, would mean a general court martial—maybe resulting in no sentence—but you can see the necessity for it. Discipline necessary for success, obeying orders—no questions asked.

That's one thing I believe should be changed, tables should be put out on sidewalks like over here. Imagine the difference in attendance if we could sit out in front of annex on a Saturday afternoon and watch 'em go by. Tres bon!

In Aunt Lettie's letter it was alleged that Mrs. Farber had sent me some candy. Never got it. I thank her just the same on behalf of some private somewhere probably who needed it worse.

*A.P.O. 714*
*311 Tank Center*
*July 26, 1918*

DEAR FOLKS,
Almost a week has passed since I wrote my last letter. I've been fairly busy, it is true, but Bud and I have been taking to hiking every evening just before dark. About a 5 km. jaunt to keep in shape. We are not getting much hardening work now.

*Renault tanks used by the American forces parked by the roadside.*
*Note the playing card designations (clubs, diamonds, etc.)*
*which indicated the Tank Corps company to which the tank belonged.*
Photograph copyright Musée de l'Armée, Paris.

I am in charge of all driving now as Longstrethe has been put on other work. It keeps one humping all morning. When new men arrive they are put thru instruction in all courses—machine gun, signalling, shop work, driving, etc. All have to qualify. Then they are assigned to companies. I take a bunch out every morning and that field is as busy as a jazz band dance. Scurrying around, up and down, about the most pleasant work of 'em all.

When we were put on the job we had to "come thru"—so we made plans and outlines of what the course would be—beautiful things and like all theory when results count, most of it had to be discarded. But when the C.O. comes around we can spring it and get away big.

This A.M. a general came out and stayed 20 to 25 minutes. He had some YMers with him. I was going good and they didn't get much chance to talk. They must have thot I invented tanks. I sent one off thru the woods and he hit a pretty large tree which did snap so he just rode up it, perpendicular almost, when it broke. Wonderful sight.

Bud and I got a 48 hour pass over Sat. and Sunday and we are going to a place near the Swiss border, tres joli and unexplored by Americans. Longstrethe is going to take a wheel some 30 miles to see a classmate. Apres la guerre, pertater [peut être] Je achête bicycle et journee en France. Like 'ell he will. You've no doubt heard what some buck said when passing the Statue of Liberty, "When I get back, old girl, if you want to see me again you'll have to turn the other way." That's me!

We have just been recommissioned in National Army—all Tankers are. So I am now 1st Lt., T.C.N.A. [Tank Corps, National Army]. Fini Artillerie, good old crossed-cannons fini. You done us dirt making us ammunition trainers, but we love you just the same.

Must go down and get my whip cord blouse from a French woman in the hamlet. She is repairing rips for me. So Long.

*Boku Love,*
*Harve*


*[Hand-printed letter to his six-year old sister, Marilee:]*

DEAR LITTLE BUNS,

I got your postal tonite. I talk to all little French girls that look like you. Some have big sticks and drive the cows and little calves out to eat grass. They stay out all day and some even knit. Last nite I was standing along the road and about 10 cows came by, a grandmother and a pretty little girl—as big as you were driving them out to eat grass. The little girl ran after it. When she came up to it she hit and hit that calf and yelled "allez" which means go on. Then she broke the stick, hitting that calf. I just laughed out loud, I said if my little Buns were here she would jump on that calf's back. Wouldn't you?

How are you? Do you get many 100's in arithmetic at kindergarten? Do you like your teacher? Don't get fresh or saucy or she may make you stay after school.

*A.P.O. 714*
*311 Tank Center*
*August 11, 1918*

DEAR ONES,

I have been under a tension ever since I got back and received letters from home and Babe all to the effect that you haven't heard from me in several weeks; and all day I have been as impatient as hell to start this letter. It's liable to be a long one. This is letter 25 with the possibility of my making a slip once in a while—so you should have received at least 22. It's a shame if any have been lost because they really are good bits, don't you know.

Bud and I left here last Tuesday but had to wait around in town until 8:30 that night for train going west. Imagine—the first leave in almost 8 months—when we could feel "absolutely nothing to do until tomorrow." We went to the barber shop and YMCA during hours that cafes are closed to Americans. We wanted to start out right. At the Y I saw two girls who are running it—who came over on the *Rochambeau* when I did. "You must have been sick," they said. "We didn't see much of you." "No, ladies, some of your YM brethren who were saloon keepers in private life used my room for a bar, feeling that their drinking in public would not be sanctioned by your organization—and I had to keep an eye on my cigarettes and other government properties."

The American Express from G.H.Q. to Tours was crowded. Officers and men ride free, but we got seats in first class compartment—and felt darned lucky as well as satisfied.

This train is made up of long continental type of cars. Porters on every car are enlisted men also American engineer and fireman. Tres bien. Every seat in our compartment was taken and our prospects were fine: 8 PM to 11 AM in one seat. Impossible to sleep or even rest. But what the hell! The others, engineer captains, for three hours told us between tears, groans and threats and sobs what they had been thru for the last month or so. They were just leaving the "Famous Raspberry Camp" [Classification Depot, near Blois, France] for officers who seem to be in need of further instructions, more comprehensive knowledge of discipline. The term varies in length depending on the subject himself, but the work is the same.

Now these officers were all captains, mind you, and from the time they got to this wonderful raspberry place they were the same as privates in every sense of word. No Sam Brownes, no bars—beaucoup guard duty (u know, as Babe wrote, 2 hours on and 4 off, clean own mess kits) like any private with the following privilege: if their shoes were dusty they got one demerit. Well, what of it? Oh, nothing except there was a big rocky slope which had to be cut away for strategic reasons. The more demerits the more chance one had to assist in levelling this off. One said he would have to be a white wing [A uniformed street cleaner] for 5 years to get his self-respect back. I mean this is what he would have said if he wanted his thots put into print.

Theirs was a wonderful tale. Joking was the only way they had to keep from going daft and committing murder. A few of their pet sayings upon the approach of the C.O. were:

> *Chief cuckoom, call out the reindeer*
> *Give 'im the mob scene (chorus of groans).*

This is just what the C.O. wanted, u see—that rock pile had to be broken up into small ones cause the big ones were too large to play with. 300 (officers) x 8 cu. ft. (one demerit) x 30 days—equals 72,000 cu. ft. minimum estimate of amount excavated. Say he came near their barracks three times a day: 3 x 72000 equals 216,000 cu ft. I laughed until I got sick. They all claimed to be the pick of their regiments sent for a little higher training—then back to the States as instructors. It must have deranged their minds. I met some later in Paris—their training had made them loco—they didn't know me. Two of them must have thot the Cafe de la Paix was the guard house and the wonderful women—sentries. They didn't leave it even at night and then they couldn't. But more about Cafe de la Paix later!

We got into Tours about noon last Wednesday, and started down the street dressed up like a Wedding with suits pressed, the only baggage was our haversacks containing a pair of socks, tooth brush and cigarettes. Eventually all my baggage won't amount to much more. Losing it continually. Might as well. Impossible to go up to the front with it as you have probably read. After and during a scrap you throw everything away. As soon as you get back or the supplies come up the gov't fits you out again, and if you come to town for a leave, buy a decent outfit. I saw officers in Tours and Paris with uniforms like privates, without insignia, Sam Brownes, etc.

I don't know why we went to Nantes. It was highly recommended but the same run of things to do. Quite a few officers there and we always strike up conversation. But unless a fellow has been wounded we fellow-tankers don't get a chance to start the bull. You never saw anything like it. Remember how romantic aviation was at first. "Let me touch you, you are an aviator's barber." That's the way the Tank corps is looked upon now. I'll bet "Black Jack" [General Pershing] would damn near apply for transfer if he wasn't afraid some sergeant mite send him Form #3X to the effect that "No further transfers are possible." Every officer we talk to listens with mouth open—wants to know if he can get in. Even those who have been up to the front. They say that we will win the war with tanks.

This is common information so I can write it: last week when the Allies drove that Chateau-Thierry salient straight, the Germans retreated like wild, but placed hundreds of machines as a rearguard to their retreat. Here then our doughboys—good old doughboys—they fight the war if anyone does—they had to advance under the machine gun fire. Mind what would have happened were there enuf tanks to go ahead and either blow up these machine gun nests or run right over them. Sanefarian [Ça ne fait rien—It doesn't matter] pour nous! why our infantry could have rested up and, well, the Rhine would be only a day away. Honestly except for artillery we don't fear a thing. I shouldn't say "fear." Artillery alone can damage us, and then it takes a direct hit—whereas anything else is like a fly on a porcupine.

We had the staff school down to see our "show" this afternoon,

*Tank Corps recruiting poster, lithographed in black and white.*
*Drawn by Sgt. Henry E. Clark*
From the collection of the Liberty Memorial Museum.

nothing under a major admitted and the other way the sky was the limit. They all went "nuts." "Wonderful! Look at that one tearing up enough wire to—run anything through. That one going along like a thoroughbred pointer after that machine gun nest."

Do you remember *Why* I transferred? My reasons:

1. The wonderful possibilities of the Tank
2. The desire for blood (grrrrr)
3. The fact that I would have a hand in it from its inception. Practically among the first in the Tank Corps of the U.S.—a unique and desirable situation
4. And, I admit, the romance of such a service which is a combination of all branches.

On our kepis we have three colors:
Red—on top
Yellow
Blue
I have a speech ready for that question which everyone asks.

Red means effectiveness of artillery
Yellow means the mobility of cavalry
Blue means the determination of infantry

I don't know, but suppose that that is the idea, because it is a fact.

I ask you what chance for the Boche when two men in a tank have fire superiority over 100 infantry. 10,000 men and 5,000 tanks over half a million men. Just like the Hebrew guard who, one night on the approach of unknown party, said "Advance, friend, with the discount." I say, "What's the percentage?" Isn't this a wonderful letter? 4 hours and not half through.

But all joking aside and apart from the inevitable feeling that a Ty Cobb has walking down Boul. Mich [Michigan Avenue in Chicago] (for that is honestly the way we are looked at) look at the cold figures. It's no more of a gamble than anything else. The casualties are not as much as infantry or artillery in the French or British Tank corps and we can do better, I'll bet. And the best of all—even if you are the unluckiest guy in the world—while I consider myself the exact opposite—you auto get yourself a couple of hundred Boche B4 going west.

Nantes, as I said before being interrupted, is like all other French cities—perhaps more ancient. Look up your Baedeker. When I get a chance I will also and see what I might have seen. But I was on leave—so I ate the best, drank Moet et Chandon [champagne], bummed around, talking with fellows from the front, etc. But it paled. We got a pass allowing us to go to La Baule—a seaside resort. But at the last minute we changed our minds—took a chance on getting to Paris without getting picked up by Provost Marshall—succeeded and got there Sunday night.

The food on the diners here is wonderful. For 7 francs we are served a meal that for tastiness and quantity I never got on diners at home, at any price. Always 4 or 5 hors d'oeuvres, veal or chicken, potatoes, wonderfully cooked vegetables, fruit, cheese, wine. Everywhere it is the same. Food Merveilleuse!

At 10 P.M. we pulled into wonderful, grand, disgustingly wicked Paris. Everyone gets verbose describing it. And I think my above paradoxical statement is correct. This is my third time. Once before the war, once on my way here and now.

At night it is quite dark on account of avions [airplanes] and it was very late before we could find a taxi. They don't run around joyriding very much. One is not allowed to taxi in the Bois de Boulogne for pleasure. I don't believe prices have been raised. One can still go 4 to 5 miles for a five franc note.

The biggest point about Paris is that except for war news in papers and every kind of uniform—one couldn't believe that the biggest war the world has seen is going on less than 75 miles away. Not much farther than Chicago Heights is from Chicago. It is almost sacrilegious—it strikes me. Of course this is true—a casual visitor doesn't see the other side. There is more life on the streets, more eating and drinking than before; and by civilians, too, altho 50% of the crowds are soldiers.

We were at the Grand Hotel and I gradually remembered little things dating back to '06. Our schedule was a late breakfast and then a front seat in front of the Cafe de la Paix. It is wonderful there. Everybody passes by or stops for a drink. Hardly ten minutes go by without seeing a friend. I met fellows continually—that I knew from high school days down to those I have known in the service. And it is always, "Have a drink" or "have another."

We ate almost every meal at the Albert cafe down past the Madeleine, managed by Jimmy, a Chicago and Frisco bartender. Three or four

Americans, who say they are bankers have always eaten there. It's a treat to hear them raise hell with the service, food, etc. But this place has no whiskey. One banker said if we would come to his hotel he would fix us up. He did with a quart of Canadian Club. I had more enjoyment the next three hours than any since I have been in France. Bud and I just consciously and deliberately went up to a hotel and got plastered. 45 francs—why it'd cost a couple of hundred to get even feeling good on French wine and stuff. We paid 10 bucks (55 francs) in Chattanooga for rot gut.

A Major who was at Tanks for a while but sent back, was in Paris. Imagine our surprise when he told us he had just come back from the line and was Major of the Motor section, 3rd Ammunition Train—our old outfit. He took Major Hunter's place. He told us the train went thru with great spirit and suffered some casualties and were out in rest now. A lot of changes have taken place. In three months the commissioned personnel will be entirely new. That's the system they use. I was sorry to hear that Capt. Shaw, in charge of casuals with us, had been killed in a motor accident, also one of the other Lts.

I am going to quit now and will continue as soon as possible. Not much over two-thirds thru. I leave you at the Cafe Albert drinking a stinger.

*Cheerio,*
*Harv*

*August 3, 1918*

DEAR FAMILY,
Here I am killing Saturday afternoon with bunk fatigue when I should be in town at the Rendezvous, Hotel de la Poste. U auto C that place Saturday and Sunday. Very few go in during the week on a/c ball games, movies, or travelling show companies at the "Y," but on those two days just about two rooms are reserved, and they all act as if the war had been over 10 years and we were reunioning. Beaucoup wine. The trucks bring us back at 9 P.M., but there are always a few who get tired, or develop headaches and the like so they just get as comfortable as they can. Hence the need for the rooms.

But I'm still here because I go on as O. D. at 5:30. I don't mind it tho except for the fact that my whipcord is being cleaned and pressed for my permission (Ah, oui. Je allay Tuesday.) The serge I bot at Sheridan was tres terrible; and the wool too heavy. So I'll look frowzy at guard mount.

Longstrethe just got back from town. French & Americans have just taken Soissons. Voila. If they'll only wait for us B4 going rite thru to Berlin. But we'll make it! Our motto in the A.E.F. now, I understand, is "Hell, heaven, or Hoboken in ? months." The first is crowded now, the second too exclusive. It must be the last. Q.E.D.

Kiss Bunsie & loads of Love,

*Harve*

*August 11—Sunday* A.M.

FOLKS,

Had a big party here last nite. Gave dinner-dance as an opener for our new Y. U. C. We are building quite a little town here, to house new batch of men we are expecting. Officially the party was given for the Colonel but, entre nous, for showing up the Staff and all in town who give weekly dances and have it understood that they are invitational affairs—without giving us any invitations. So we just crabbed their whole affair by corralling all the Signal corps girls and nurses and showing them what a real party is like.

Our camouflage artist spent a lot of time on it. It looked like a grotto. Five tanks were put at disposal of crowd and all the girls had a ride. The fight lasted until midnite. The girls went home in 5 ton trucks. You have to admit it's a hard war.

The best part of the whole thing was that after 9 months I have had an opportunity of wearing that white shirt which Mater or Aunt Annie so thotfully and carefully packed in my locker. I found the shirt and, Imagine! it was even complete with collar and cuff buttons. I kept great care of my boots, soaping them continually, even have them hanging on the wall; like a Rembrandt, a classic of art. They were so wonderful that whenever I got low, a fond look at them would work wonders. And it got so that when any of the Buddies were low they went in and looked at them, too, with the same result. You auto see those boots now! Still the same source of satisfaction, as soft as cloth and as comfortable as house slippers and as beautiful as mahogany. Funny, what a little drink'll do?

I was in the Cafe Albert drinking a stinger when I left you in my last letter. At about 3:30 P.M. we'll go to the Cafe de la Paix—U C the whole scheme is not to move around any more than is necessary because there is no use drinking a million francs worth of stuff a day if you are going to waste it on pure air. Being a Tanker I can talk authoritatively— never sink so low in the dregs that you become rational. Is not the right thing to do! The test of a true Tanker is this: can he recognize his friends? If so, he is weakening and must take suitable steps if he can and stock up again. Another and more difficult test is to be able to go to the Casino de Paris or Folies Bergere with some brother officers and leave in the same suitable company without any Parisian additions of Paquin or Marguerite.

One gets so disgusted at the actions of these women. They are dolled up like the cover of *Vogue* and they represent 50% of every crowd. They walk up and down the main 'drags' like at a fashion show with all kinds of dogs and after a few hours you've got to get "cuckooed" to keep from beating them up.

At the Casino or the Folies they are even worse. By that time, after 8 p.m. they begin getting wild from lack of food. It's a cinch they haven't eaten since noon. Between acts especially, and for that matter all during the show they promenade coyly about with their "Hello, Dearie, are you lonesome?" etc. They know enough English to strike an offended attitude when you tell them to "go to hell." All cafes close at 9:30 and no drinks served after that publicly—but there are plenty of Q.T. places for all hours.


*A.P.O. #714*
*311 Tank Center*
*August 21, 1918*


Dear Ones,
I must tell you of the pleasant surprise I had this morning. As usual I was out giving instructions in tank driving—a sort of finishing course to men who have already been thru the preliminary way. A general's car drove up. You can always tell them, a white star or stars on a red background on the windshield. At a distance, I recognized Gen. Smith [Brig. Gen. Harry A. Smith, commander of the AEF schools in France]. He has sort of adopted the Tank corps, as he calls on me at the driving field many times a week. Accompanying him were two other men in khaki. One was a Lt., the general's aide, and the other was Mr. Rosenwald.

As they came nearer I clicked the old heels together and "nicked" the general hard. It's old stuff with me to get clubby with the big boys! I have seen too many "reserve" officers act as tho they were going to slap a superior on the back and call him by his nickname rather than salute properly and stand at attention and then eat in civil life. And that's going some, n'est-ce pas?

The general says, says he, "Lt. Harris (I told you we were 50-50, comme çi, comme ça) "this is"—not being a military guy the aforesaid Mr. broke in—absolutely interrupted the general with "For goodness sake's, Harris. How are you? Saw your folks not long ago and they are all fine. Why, general, he was one of our best men at the University." "He is one of our best men here, too. I come out to see him often here," quoth the general.

This was beginning to get my goat so I carried on with, "Sir, is it your wish to have a tank manoeuvre for Mr. Rosenwald?" He said it was so I got my best sergeant and told him to take the shell holes, trenches and then hit for the woods-about 300 meters away. Dammed if it didn't go swell, just like a circus horse and I felt like the trainer receiving the plaudits of the audience. I had an opportunity to ask Mr. Rosenwald how he liked it—that I had noticed his name in arrivals in Paris, how long he expected to be over? "Fine, Yes, and 2 or 3 months." Just then the tank hit a tree at the edge of the woods, went up on end and then disappeared. "He's tipped over," yelled Mr. R. I said, "We'll go over and

*Extra supplies, including packages, helmets, rope and barrels, were transported on the back side of the Renault tank.*
Photograph copyright Musée de l'Armée, Paris.

see." We went. Tipped over, Hell! It was moving thru, riding over stumps, trees, walls and everything. Then it backed out just as easily. "Sight of a lifetime," said Mr. J.R. and even the general got ecstatic.

Then Longstrethe came up and I introduced him. Between us we got a suit of overalls (black with grease) and managed to get our guest into the critter without banging his head or cutting him up. He stood up acting as gunner and the sergeant gave him a ride over the course. When he got back he said it was a great experience and I asked if he had taken the shell holes and trenches. He had, altho he had a darn good driver who minimized every bump, believed he was a little "leary," and while bracing and holding on he had forgotten to look out of the slits to see where he was going. But he got the sensation. "I'll write to your folks at once and tell them I have seen you—good luck and thank you, Lt." Another good "nick" for the general and finis! When I turned back to the tanks they were standing "dressed up" like a bunch of cars in a garage—ready to start out on platoon drill in a straight line, military as 'ell—looked like a prearranged plan to make an impression. Nothing of the kind! A well organized course at 10:35 A.M. line-up for 40 minute drill—regular schedule. Nothing like getting away big or even kidding yourself that you are.

*Paris, August 25th, 1918*

DEAR MR. AND MRS. HARRIS,

It was a real joy for me to see your fine boy—Capt. Harris—at Langres on Wednesday last. He is a handsome chap, and the picture of health. His General, who escorted me, told me that he had noticed him as being a very good soldier and always on the job. He gave me a ride in a tank, which was an interesting experience.

My congratulations to you both upon having raised such a fine fellow. You have reason to be proud of him.

*Cordially,*

*Julius Rosenwald,*
*President of Sears*
*Roebuck*

*Saturday*
*September 5, 1918*

It has been 10 days since my last letter and I'm really fortunate to be able to write now—where I've been there has been no stationery—no time during day—no light at night. Well, where have you been Mr. Whitewash? Why all this secrecy among friends? Can't say, all I ask is that you will be patient and wait until I can rite fully. Be content with just a note "now & then." My 20 pages about my permission will hold until the next big one, and when she comes—wow—I am keeping notes for it, tous les jours.

I haven't seen a newspaper for a couple of weeks but understand British are doing wonders. I suggest you keep newspapers and special dope.

That I am again wearing artillery insignia but with a special title of "Special Engineer" tends only to complete the quandary you must be in. Think of Imy and Aunt Lettie—how desirous they must be to know.

But now that I have you completely off the scent I say "wait" and you shall hear.

I am fine and having an experience that many do not get and I really believe that because my last bath was in August sometimes only adds to my healthy state.

Continue sending my mail to the same A.P.O. I do not know how long this present work will continue—but until a successful culmination I am sure. As soon as possible I will cable you and send my complete serial.

Now listen, it may be a little long between drinks—but don't worry. And with beaucoup beaucoup love and a big kiss administered by every one on little Buns,—from me.

*Devotedly,*
*Harvey*

# 4

## TWO
## BIG SHOWS

TANK CORPS

TREAT EM' ROUGH

*Sunday*
*Sept. 15, 1918*

My Dear Ones,

I have had no time to write—much as I have had to say. You, no doubt this morning (which I hope is as beautiful at home as it is here) are reading about our first practically all-American success. Fine, isn't it? The ole bells auto be ringing now!

I do not want to start my story now, because any minute we may get orders to move over the top. But I have beaucoup notes, and when I do get time—wow! It will take a week to write it. Incidentally this is Boche paper, and I am writing now in a room occupied by some damned Dutchman not many hours ago, and where same guy probably held forth for four years. Just think these people have had Boche here for 4 years—and when we came thru not long after our infantry their actions and expressions were indescribable. Dazed, Silent! I'll never forget it and in my leisure sometimes I'll try to describe it more.

I have seen so much in the last 10 days prior to attack and since— that no one letter can hold. The preparation, the attack with its artillery accompaniment—the bringing up of everything to new positions, men wounded, horses killed, evacuation of this town by civilians, wonderful! Awful! Never before have I really known the real meaning of the word "awful."

Interruption—French Captain just came in. Je parle, "Pas de Nouvelles?" "Oui, nous revenir." Anyway outfit we R attached to is being relieved. We go back a little. Don't misunderstand! Our line is advancing a little all the time altho there is no concerted action. Perhaps now that this salient is wiped out there, there is no need of pushing on. Bad weather will soon come and it is hard to imagine what it means to bring up everything necessary, following an attack which was so fast as this one—over bad roads. It had rained continually for 4 days.

Altho I would jump at opportunity to go on—it has however, been almost 3 weeks since I have taken off my clothes—no change of anything with me—so why go to trouble to take anything off? For about 6 nites I slept under trees or in a truck—if lucky enuf to find one broken down. Everything that could move—moved, believe me.

Except for fact that every time I move I find a new place to scratch (and it is some satisfaction to be able to find that new place) I'm feeling

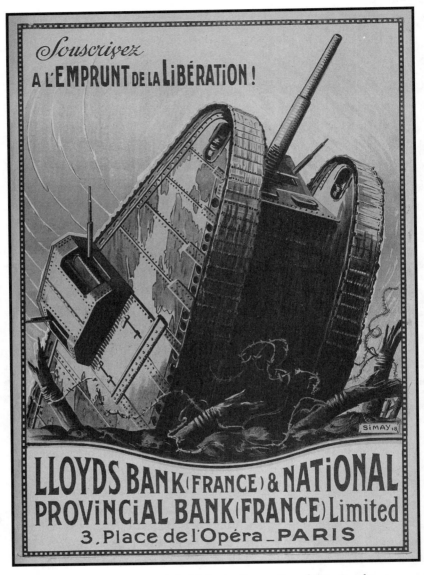

*"Souscrivez à l'Emprunt de la Libération" was a French War Bond poster*
*designed by Simay, in 1918.*
Photograph copyright Musée de l'Armée, Paris.

great. Couldn't be better. Some days 3 meals—some days a piece of Loos Wiles hard bread—2 days nothing but water! Get used to it all. C'est la guerre.

You should have seen this place a few hours ago—well say the morning following our taking it—(We took it at noon of 1st day). Everybody looking for souvenirs, left by Boche. Helmets, guns, boots, everything. One of our infantry companies which was in reserve was lined up in front of a Boche supply room outfitting itself with heavy underwear, socks and anything else they wanted. The only thing I really have wanted was a German pistol. Couldn't find one. Helmets, rifles, leather gas masks, bayonets, etc., etc. laying around in buildings—on streets where perhaps one of shells wrecked a wagon—and in fields. I did get a little thing cut out of some limestone which will be a nice thing for your curio cabinet, Mater, comme ça! It is about 4 inches high and I will try and send it to you. But I feel unless there is something particularly good or interesting about a thing or unless perhaps a personal value—say 4 instance 100 Boche after me alone and I get them all with about 40 shots in which case I might take their iron crosses, it is useless to try and carry a lot of junk around. Mite as well buy it when I get back to States. N'est-ce pas?

Good, our artillery has just arrived back of the town. All morning the Boche have been shooting 'em in—now our batteries are opening up and it is well. With no trenches our infantry has been hard put for the last two days—under continual shelling out in the open, digging in with mess kits or anything they had and no artillery assistance. Fortunately few severe casualties—just shrapnel wounds.

Oh, the Boche are finis! I don't know what has happened the last few weeks but just from rumors the English and French have been hitting them for a homer, continually. Nothing much this winter—but next Spring! OOh la la! I'd hate even to have one of Pater's Russian rubles bet on them to last next Spring out.

So since we're not going on, let's call it "quits"—and in a few days I hope to cable and also write a full account!

A bath!

Hot water to soak my shoes off!

Regular meals!

And a sheltered nook to keep out the everlasting rain!

Oh, A.P.O. #714, like heaven now! If you think a month of it isn't long enuf—for awhile at least—ask me, I know.

Yours in haste and with much love,

*Harvey*

P.S. Now, don't worry about no mail—after the next show without a doubt we'll return to rest billet or same A.P.O. number then U'll hear from us.

On a/c of moving around so much, too, I had only had 3 or 4 letters from you. That's the hard part of it! and they came all in a bunch, too. I take that back—just yesterday I got one from Mater—with facsimile of my T.C. commission—why—for a letter from home even food has no counter attraction!

I wish I could get a paper or so and see what is happening particularly in other parts of this sector. And I do hope that you can keep a file of papers and any interesting dope U can get on it—First American Drive—and to think I'm fortunate enuf to have been in on it! Long before the start, and to see all preparations! With passes to circulate anywhere—and circulate I did.

I wish I could get time to write you all my experiences now, but I think U will wonder about some things.

1st - Haven't a scratch (i.e. inflicted except by own hands—oh the cooties or the dirt or other diverse bugs are terrible). I've had one man wounded from shrapnel—under my charge, when the Boche saw my working party one day B4 the attack—and on day of attack I had a shrapnel pellet hit me on the leg—stung like a stone and that's all.

Here's a good one—A Lieut. was wounded—another officer asked this Lieut's. sergeant—"was he wounded, badly?" "Oh no, only a wound stripe!"

2nd - Haven't got a Boche yet—nearest I came was one day when I was out on patrol on my own, studying the topography of Boche lines—I think I saw a Boche running down a trench about 20 ft. from me—I know I saw his coat tail go around a corner—and I continued my reconnaissance—after waiting for 10 minutes or so for him or any of his friends to "show." If you think it isn't a funny feeling try it. Walk out the trench past your own forward observation post and at every turn expect to see the enemy coming your way.

3rd - Only thing I need is cigarettes and none are to be had around here. I have 1500 in my trunks at A.P.O. 714. That's the way it always happens. But I'll make it some way.

I have a swell billet here. Just a common white building from the front just like all the others,—but thru a gate and up a flight of stairs and the prettiest little garden! My room is just off this garden. A wonderful old lady lives here and this morning she made us an 8 egg omelet pour les deux. And last nite the moon shown rite thru the door on to my bed.

Now my Cherie, bon soir, with much love.


*September 18, 1918*
*Somewhere in France*

MY FIRST BATTLE
Part 1

MY DEAR ONES,
At last, after almost a month of strenuous life it is with a great deal of pleasure that I am going to try and recount my experiences. For a day or so at least, it seems, we will rest here, and it has been a long time since I have anticipated a few days' rest—with so much satisfaction.

In Mater's last letter she wrote of the regular summer evening sessions out on the lawn with ice cream to top off a hot day. It was a great picture. I hope these accounts—it may be 3 or 4 letters will be necessary to finish them—will reach you during one of those sessions, and that you will get as much enjoyment out of them as I did—both in actuality and in writing them to you.

My only worry has been that my cigarettes wouldn't hold out, but now with a Package still left, out of 500 that I started with the 25th of last month—and my stock replenished this morning even to the extent of a box of cigars—a wonderful sleep last nite, four meals straight without a miss (you'll understand later why I mention this about the meals) I am "sitting pretty."

I've been in the First Big American Drive—for two weeks before it began until now that it is, I presume, over. This salient was straightened out nice as you please in about five hours time; and I'm going to start at the beginning and tell you what I did, saw and thot during that time. If it gets tiresome skip a hundred pages or so—and begin again.

So let's go!

About August 20th or so the dope came around that some officers were going to the Allied Tank School near where Babe is situated and I was very hopeful that I could get to go to see Babe and get the change, also. But I was instructing in driving. There evidently was no one else— so Bud, Longstrethe and others left and I was to go the next week. In the meanwhile with my two buddies gone and I alone in the hut—I was resigned to a damned hard week.

On Saturday the 24th, I stayed around all day. Didn't go to town with the Tankers and help them keep up our reputation—which is fast becoming nation-wide—I believe I wrote a few letters, then went down to an old French woman and arranged to buy 2 chickens from her with French fries and some wine. We were going to have a swell mid-nite lunch. This was about 5:30. When we got back a Lt. said, "Meeting with Colonel at 6:30. I've had a hell of a time breaking up beer parties all afternoon in town, rounding up all you birds. I'll bet I'm the most unpopular guy in the Tank Corps." Someone had seen the Colonel with artillery insignia and red stripe on kepi. What could that mean?

You know the French Tanks are a part of the Artillery. Maybe that's what's going to happen to us—lose our identity. Well, there was great expectancy for the next hour. What's the dope? Then some fellow would come out of a hut with a knowing expression and pretending he had it straight from G.H.Q., would tell us some wild stuff that he'd probably thot of while shaving.

The Colonel [George S. Patton, Jr.] talks in a high voice and, sort of without any connection, he jumped rite into discussing how he'd court-martial anyone who said anything about arrivals, departures, etc., that if the tank gets put out of commission the only place for officers to be found is with their machine guns in front line of infantry, otherwise we were not doing our duty and mite as well not have been born.

It was a rousing talk, but there was no connection between it and anything we knew.

During dinner two lists were circulated, one being list of officers of the 2 battalions to meet the Major at 7:30 P.M.—the other a list of unassigned officers—of which I was one—none of officers instructing were assigned to either Battalion—to report at 7 P.M.

I wasn't on either list! And taking a nose count I saw that only 4 or

5 others were in same shape as I was—on neither list. Pourquoi? Just like not getting a commission on last day of camp. But still no one knew what the meetings were about! So I waited for some of either list to come back from the meetings. A man waiting to get married couldn't have felt any differently than I did. It's a cinch something is up!

Then a couple of them drifted back down the street—but no signs of recognition. They knew how anxious I was—but nary a word. "What, you're not going to tell me—me what's been your friend?"

"We're going away from here," and that's all they would say—and began to pack. One asked me for my revolver and gas mask. He is the one who was just transferred from a colored Q.M. labor regiment. Well they must be going up to the Front, probably will see our first American drive, see our tanks operate, actually get into the war which I've read and thot of and worked for, for over a year—and I am to stay behind.

Now Mater, withhold your remarks please for a few moments. This has got to be done with complete gestures. I never thot of what you are thinking of. But hark!

They begin packing, and then comes a low conversation—presumably about what equipment to take. I watched them from my bunk: trench knives and clean sheets, white shirts and revolvers. Don't you see, they don't go together. One mite for Paris, the other at the Front. I saw it was useless to question them—so I rolled up and tried to sleep. But the terrible thot, surmise, that perhaps they're going up to Front and are going to get into the war—prevented any sleep. Y the damned war will be over B4 I get near it! That'd be swell, wouldn't it?

Then an orderly came in with an order for me to the effect that beginning Monday, August 26th, classes for Tank driving would report to me at 7:30 A.M. That was a little consolation. They needed me there—I was really the only one who had been instructing in driving. How could they send me away, too? Then the adjutant came in and I asked him Y in 'ell I wasn't "in on the party whatever it was, whether they're going to the States or the Front." "I'll tell you that we need you here for driving instructor." I growled, and went to sleep, dreaming of going over with tanks and of pulling into New York harbor, alternatively.

At 6:25 the next morning the adjutant came into the hut. I had the canvas flap pulled up over my face. I was still sore at the world. He asked, "who's this!" I wouldn't answer him on a bet so he pulled the flap back, looked at my cherubic countenance, and went out. Three minutes later he rushed back in. "Dragit out, quick," he said. "Did U Pass the Reconnaissance course (I, who took all the geology and geography the University of Chicago offered, had specialized in it for years—did I pass their Reconnaissance course)? "Hell, Yes." "Good, get up, U're going to the Front. The truck is waiting now, and everyone else is ready, make it snappy!" he said.

Imagine my feelings! I didn't have a chance to get elated as we must be on our way in 20 minutes. Dress, grab breakfast and pack. That's fine! I never dressed faster or ate with less desire for food. Then the question was, what to take? That auto be easy. I've been buying equipment for almost a year and a half. I must have everything I can possibly need. How long'll we be gone. Don't know! Well the first thing is that carton of 500 Lucky Strikes—then a couple pairs of socks, an extra shirt, a towel, shaving outfit, guns, gas mask, 2 pencils—all this in my haversack. Then, in addition to my bedding roll, $8.00 worth of stuff out of at least $500.00 to pick from.

Note particularly now what equipment I took, and let everyone else be governed likewise. I've gone almost a month now with that list—and am still able to continue. It's ridiculous to have too much, one just can't bother with it. Everytime I had to move I put my revolver belt on, sling on my haversack—and went. The more you have—the more you lose or willfully throw away.

At 6:50 A.M. we were on the road in a Riker limousine, you know one of those 3 ton babies: 8 lieutenants and 2 captains. The one of the latter who was in charge probably knew where we were going—but no one else did. They were a happy bunch, no matter where we were going, there was going to be a few days change of scene at any rate—and as long as a soldier moves he doesn't care a whoop where he is going. It's the confounded drag of sitting in one place—no matter the conveniences, that wrecks the morale.

At first when we pulled thru the town nearest us—the same one we always go to whenever we can get transportation—it looked as tho we were going to take a train—and since it was such a beautiful morning—none of us wanted that.

But we stopped only to get our orders which the Captain had stamped, and were off again. We had chuck [food] with us—and not knowing how long we'd be on the way—all tried to keep from eating any. Pretty soon one bird opened a box of hard bread; the rest of us got peeved. "Save that food." "Save, Hell," he said. If that's the feeling then let's go to it. And everyone grabbed. Cans of corn wooley [corned beef] disappeared toute suite—and it was continual eatfest the rest of the way. Officers or enlisted men are all alike. If that had been 4 days rations and if we knew full well that it had to last us, too—we'd have cleaned up most of it the first day, irrespective and notwithstanding. Like the men Syke and I brot over who ate 4 days allowance of jam at their first meal.

That noon we arrived at good sized city on way up to this sector. If you look at the map you may get an idea what one it is. About half way from A.P.O. 714 to this Front. Now that U know perfectly where it is, I'll tell you we ate at the Lafayette Club, which is an officers'—(French & American) Club. It sits back about 200 ft. from street, in a beautiful garden and was patronized by a large number of officers. The whiskey flips were wonderful and the food fair. We only remained there long enuf to eat, and to a keen observer we must have been or made a queer combination, on account of the insignia we wore. Not a Tanker in the bunch. All had been instructed to take off tank insignia and hat colors before leaving. So there we were—Artillery, Engineers, Infantry, Quartermaster, Signal Corps, etc. All presumably bound on the same mission. Does that explain the reason for our Colonel's wearing Artillery insignia? No? Camouflage! If we were to be successful no one must know we're around, not even our own Infantry officers. "And don't act the part of the smart guy either," warned the Colonel. "And think you've got to act the part of a general trying to keep his plans secret."

At about 6 in the evening we arrived at first destination. At least where we were to report for orders. It was at one edge of a large camp—where we saw many of our first divisions to get into action on the west front—in repose. It had been an awful hard ride, and of course as we passed thru town after town we quickly figure where we were going. Several of the men had been here with Infantry outfits when it was a quiet sector and I knew the country well. Just B4 end of trip we passed an immense tent and hut field hospital going up and except for that there was nothing else indicative of our approach to a battle front. Of course we were still 30 km from it, and it is very quiet anyway.

After supper we reported to another Colonel who was to be our chief while on this work. We were divided into four groups of 2 to a group. St. Burgess and myself had assigned to us the right sector, each was given a map, very meagre instructions, except that we were to form reconnaissance parties—go over our sector, get to know it well, and reports to be left at our billet or at whatever Headquarters we would make our Hqs.—to be picked up daily by motorcycle and Chief Reconnaissance officer, a captain.

In other words: "Here is your sector, from here to here, you R going to have so many tanks, how R U going to get them up to the line, and then what and how are you going to handle them."

"That's all. The truck will leave at 7 in the morning to take U all to your respective places. Results count." Nick em hard, about face and walk out. That's what we did. He's a hard bird, n'est-ce pas? And since we've reaffirmed that many times. So tomorrow we actually get into the field!

May continue letter in afternoon.

*Lots of love,*
*Harv*

*September 18, 1918*
*Somewhere in France*

### Part 2

After a lapse of a few hours I am going to continue.

Our new C. O. gave us only most meagre information. "Results count," he said. "You are to go out as special engineers and no one under rank of corps commander or general staff officer is to know what you are doing around."

So early next morning we were all up early, but not early enuf to see a Boche plane flying around over the camp and our anti-aircraft guns open up on him. They didn't get him. We started towards the left of our entire sector and in pairs we were dropped off at various regimental headquarters—which for time being at least we were to attach ourselves to. Here, then, was our situation: Not even tell brigadier generals what our mission was. On our passes one General Staffer wrote, "On important business—not to be asked any questions, but given all assistance." So all day we skirted along parallel to the front. Each side had four or five observation balloons up, our planes in groups or singly would fly by—but all in all it was almost impossible to realize that perhaps not more than 4 or 5 km. away were our and the Boche lines. No shooting, except a machine gun now and then—at a plane. More like going to a baseball game. Since then my views have changed. I've seen considerable in the last three weeks—but even at that—it all struck me as being just a big, grand spectacle, carefully rehearsed. No cavalry racing like mad over dead-strewn fields—or the like—nothing but what seemed absolutely planned and agreed to by both sides. That's the way it struck me in a big way. Perhaps because it seemed so cut and dried like, viz., after infantry captured an area or moved on, what happened then? Why the artillery—especially lighter guns begin moving up—after them, what? The men must eat, the guns require ammunition; i. e., supplies must come up immediately—hence because it worked out just this way might be reason for our being so easily, entirely successful.

Late in the afternoon we were dumped off at a corps Hqs. Not a billet in the town. Twice as many officers there as could be well accommodated "Ça ne fait rien pour nous," we'll supper here, and with your transportation we'll go on to Brigade Hqs. tonite—the nearer up we get, the better. So after supper around comes a beautiful pearl-upholstered, Winton Six, (you know the kind U stop and look at on Boul. Mich., [Michigan Avenue, in Chicago] or that pulls up to the Opera.) Rite then we both decided that a general's job is the "nuts." They get billets that a Chicago millionaire couldn't even enter in peacetime—palaces— everything in place. That's one thing you find in general. All fixtures, ornaments, etc., out just as when owners lived in them. Here's the dope. Every house is considered a billet, and in towns anywhere near troops, there is a board on every house:

| | |
|---|---|
| Chev. | 8 |
| H. | 40 |
| O. | 2 |

Meaning:

| | |
|---|---|
| Horses | 8 |
| Men | 40 |
| Officers | 2 |

So when billetting officer of any outfit comes ahead of outfit to arrange for quarters, he knows just what to count on. Hence C. O. is bound to get best billet—and best in any town or village is at least passing fair. In some places you can well imagine the grandeur: Probably Dukes' and Marquis' mansions which tourists visited in peacetimes just on a/c of their wonders.

It was only 5 or 6 km. to Brigade Hqs., but the sensation was a lasting one. Every soldier and officer, no matter the rank, would snap up and salute as we passed by. Then I could almost feel their disgust when they perhaps saw we were only 1st Lts. I know their feelings only too well. How many times have I "nicked" [salute] even an empty car that had a general's star or two on it. But the funniest thing along this line was when one of our 2nd Lts. grabbed a Major General's car one day back at _____ and who should he pass but our Colonel—who stiffened up and saluted most grandly. He's most military, anyway.

At Brigade Hqs.,—in a dark unpretentious building was the General of the Brigade [Brigadier General Samuel D. Rockenbach.] He was there alone. At first sight he looked the image and had the actions of Uncle Barney. We got to know him wonderfully well—so much so that he told us of his plans. He had had 23 fights in the Philippines and elsewhere and had always used men—no matter how many were required—but now he was all for using machinery. That's where we came in. We always had entree to his office—while everyone else waited and towards the end when they found out what we were there for—everyone was most eager for our dope which we gave only sparingly.

But it was late that nite when we reported—the town major couldn't be found, and after signing our names for comparison with our signatures on passes—the question was: Where to sleep?

The only place was a sheet iron lean-to, a chicken coop arrangement next to Headquarters, two sides boarded, one with chicken netting, no floor but the ground. I'll tell the world—it was quite a comedown; Winton Six and Generals to a chicken coop. But for two days we had pounded the roads in that Riker—and with bedding rolls—we could sleep anywhere. I had that rubber sheet on bottom next to my blankets, and that together with canvas should keep out dampness.

Examining roof, I put my roll in what I thot a strategic location, in case of rain, took off my shoes and slept—I don't know for how long—but I was rudely awakened by water dropping first in my left eye, then in my mouth. It was pitch dark, cold and raining—no candle or light of any kind around either. I worked roll to port about 20 degrees and went to sleep again without any trouble. But U'll admit it was a compromising situation—when I've always claimed I don't snore to excess, to have rain pouring into my mouth.

In the morning I looked the situation over—where my mouth was, there was the only leak in the whole shed.

War or no war—the first thing we considered absolutely necessary in the morning was to eat. To wash was not so important. The next three weeks taught us that often both were sometimes impossible. Dressing, I mean putting on my shoes and inhaling a cigarette. How wonderful that first cigarette of a morning tastes when U inhale it down to your toes! We discussed the question of where to eat. Thompson's is quicker, but the Blackstone coffee is wonderful! [Thompson's was a low-cost restaurant in Chicago, while the Blackstone was an elegant hotel.]

So we started out for the officers' mess. We hit the place to which we'd been directed. First ones there. Then the mess officer came in. "Can we make arrangements to eat here for a few days perhaps?" "It mite be alrite," he said, "but this is the general's private mess." You'll see later that generals didn't mean much to us—but this was our initiation—and sort of taken back we started on orderly withdrawal, fairly well armed with thot that we belonged at that mess just the same—sort of superior—like travelling under orders of G.H.Q. secret business!

Then the door opened, and in came the grizzled old Gen. himself—Fighting Patsy—he's called. "Won't you sit down, gentlemen?" "If it's not intruding, sir." "Not at all!" So we had our first mess with a general. The general made us feel perfectly at home. And that's another thing. I found thru experience that holds good in the army as well as in business—the higher up you can go the more attention and better success you can get. If U can get by the fellows that are put there to keep you from getting by to see the chief, the further along U can get.

But with all apologies to Patsy, his breakfast was rotten in its lack of quantity—one egg, coffee and a piece of toast. Must be purely brain food—certainly lacking in protein for a reconnoitering party!

We started out then, Tuesday morning, armed with gas masks, gats, maps, and passes to go anywhere. "Circulate in the area" is the way they read.

But of this we were decided; they can't fox us out of going and seeing the front line—which we heard of and read of for four years—unless they work pretty damned fast—for we're going up there first crack—and we started walking the shortcut way about 3-5 Kms.

### First Day in Front Line Trenches

As we walked along we remarked on the nature of the ground, and that it was this quite rugged country with relief of 100 ft. or so that naturally made this quiet sector. If there was an object in taking it, and if men didn't count, it could be taken easily. But at many bends in ravines one machine gun could stand off a regiment. Units shot up in other more important sectors need a place to go and be built up and rest. For this reason then, the nature of the topography and the fact that France was in no condition to make an offensive here alone—the Boche had no objection—all connected in making it a nice quiet place.

The first thing we had noticed as we moved up was a sign something like this "on voit Saucisse." [German observation balloon, in the shape of a sausage.] That was too much French for us. It might have meant "Sausage for Sale" for all of us. If we had been more careful three or four days later and had heeded that sign we would not have brought artillery fire down on our working party. But then as it turned out one engineer would be without a wound stripe today, and they don't get many chances to get them.

That sign meant "The balloon sees you" and when we came up to a National Highway that ran northward into Boche land, some men told us about where the German lines were, and pointed out their balloons.

We were on an open swell, and there stretched out below both to right and left were the trenches, nothing to show where ours ended or where the Boche began. Not a soul to be seen anywhere. Nothing but trenches leading everywhere and up to woods 1000 meters away directly ahead. From our view the whole thing looked absolutely devoid of life, just as if we were looking down on a small clay model. True, we could point out definitely that the Boche must be from there and north of that line—because their lines were shown on our maps; and we could also see that in those trenches were beaucoup soldiers—eagerly watching each other—we could say it, but think how unsatisfactory an impression for a first one! How different from old time warfare, out in the open. Hell's-Bells there's nothing exciting about that—might as well be back in the S. A. S. Yes? Wait and see!

Shortly we came to a few troops on the reverse side of a crest in a woods who directed us to their company P. C. (Poste de commande) where commanding officer holds forth. The captain wasn't there, he'd gone ahead to his observation station on the point of the crest.

There he was looking out thru a camouflaged window of a little shed.

*September 22, 1918*
*On the way to some other place*

We showed the captain our credentials and very solicitously he walked back to show us entrance to his trenches. It was Bayou Rappe. It led down one slope of a valley which ran parallel to the lines and up the other. Just as we started up the other side, we met two lieutenants to whom we explained we were on some special engineering work that necessitated our getting the best view of no man's land. I hope it was necessary to get the best view—to lay out routes for each tank over Yankee land—(no man's land) because there was the damnedest system of trenches I could imagine.

DOMMIERS (JUILLET 1918).

Dessin de M. Durieux.

*A battlefield scene, with a Renault tank, at Dommiers, July, 1918,*
*from a drawing by M. Durieux.*
Illustration copyright Musée de l'Armée, Paris.

To have any kind of an idea of the trenches here, you must bear in mind that the lines have seen little activity for all these four years. The Boche advanced down there at the very beginning—practically the first few days with a view of taking in the French iron mines at Briey—which, of course, they did. Then for several years there was no change. The sector, as you know was always called quiet and was used for training areas.

When gas came into vogue the French found themselves holding a line which was in the lower areas, and hence bad on a/c of gas attacks (which the Boche did regularly) so the French drew back a kilometer or so.

Well, what was the result? The Boche did not advance and take the system the French had left for same reason French had considered it pas bon; so all along this salient then you had a no man's land from 300 to 1000 metres across—all interspersed with trenches, bayous, etc., where both sides had a machine gun now and then, and forward observation posts.

The tanks then at the outset of the attack would have to cross all these trenches even before coming to the Boche resistance. Hence reason for our attempting to lay out a route for each tank so as to get away from crossing as many trenches as possible. To do this even observation from our front lines would be of little good. It is necessary to go out between the lines, to be able to look back, etc.

You can see how easy it would be to start out a perfectly nice looking trench in our lines and walk rite into the Boche land.

You must also bear in mind that for four years both sides had had ample opportunity to dig wonderful wide trenches—with tank traps, etc. And, Mister, were they wide? Eight to ten feet across and same depth. And the rock sub-soil was a poorly consolidated shaley limestone, which in rain would become oozey mud. Worst kind of ground imaginable—without even considering abnormalities of trenches.

With these thots in mind then let us suppose we met these lieutenants, one was sitting with a sergeant with automatic drawn looking down a bayou leading out to the left. OO la la! Pourquoi? Several times Boche patrols had slipped over here—leaving their own lines by a sap [A side trench, perpendicular to the main trench] and following trenches to our lines. This Lt. was either hoping to get a prisoner should such a patrol come around or else was a "little" worried and felt safer with his gun in hand. They told us they had an advanced day post where we could get a good view.

So we started out to look for this post. All along the way we'd lay over edge of trench and take a look at lay of the land. A lot of wire and heavy swelling topography!

We didn't pass a soul or hear a sound. Snooping along with "Gats" at full cock we went really expecting to run into Boche at every turn of trench. At several bends we pushed aside some barb wire which obstructed the entire trench. And here is where we showed our greatest ignorance—for those entanglements meant "Don't take this trench—it leads to Boche land." But we were old timers—to exaggerate—up to that time—during our entire military careers—we'd spent about 18 minutes in honest to goodness fighting trenches. And here we were pushing aside these most effective means of good advice, viz., 4 point 8 gauge barbed wire and walking on.

But at this time tho remember we were looking for that post of observation and we mite have very easily—well, I'd say we had about 80% chance, rite then of seeing Boche—been within 100 metres of the Boche lines.

It was oppressingly quiet. U know the kind that comes just B4 a heavy black storm, when even the leaves don't move! With nothing to annoy us we slid up and looked back to our lines—of course from one trench it is almost impossible to see the next—unless you want to make a good target for a sniper—but what we did see sent the "creepers" all over. The town 500 to 700 metres directly back of us was Faye-en-Haye! For God's sake where are we? Faye-en-Haye is 200 metres out in no man's land. A look at our map and one look is enuf! We are within a stone's throw of the Boche lines—700 metres from our own.

How we got there, or why we didn't go the other way when we started from Hqs. that morning? Mite get a chance to get a prisoner tho! Oui, Oui, Oui! But U must remember we are not a combat patrol—we're just reconnoiterers.

Our minds were working about a mile a minute, and without any discussion whatsoever we started to go back.

I had visions of capturing a Boche at every turn of trench; of spending some months at some German watering place—with no food. How you all would feel when U heard I'd got a Croix de Guerre [French military medal] for single-handed capture of a Boche general!

In the meantime, mind ye, we were moving pretty fast to the rear! No matter how small a stone one of us would scrape it and it would sound like a land slide. Our helmets would hit things and would ring like a bell. If the trench had been four feet wider we would have scraped the sides anyway. Oh! it was wonderful, even the orderly retreat!

It was really thrilling—and so far we were the only actors—comedians doing a pantomime!

Just one (1) year to the day (August 27th) since I had gone wearily back for the second Training Camp.

Then a French plane approached, its flight paralleling our lines. It was flying very low—so that one could distinguish the occupants. Our second sensation was near!

As he flew about over our heads a Boche machine gun opened up on him—with bursts of 15–20 shots each. I haven't heard anything that sounds as mean as a machine gun with its regular, rat-tat-tat-tat (3 or 4 per second) shooting.

But our plane was moving rite along not a bit worried. As soon as he got out of range of this gun—the next would let loose on him—and so on all along. Sometimes 2 or 3 would be firing on him at once.

By this time Boche anti-aircraft opened up on him—and he took for higher levels. As many as 20 white blotches wud appear at one time, then as the explosions came to us we knew at about what range those guns were shooting—count the seconds from the white puff until we got the sound of the explosion. Sound travels 1100 ft. a second.

But they didn't worry him—always broke where he'd been interrupted for purpose of taking proper measures against that damned French itch.

Several times later in afternoon we saw similar target work on our planes, by the Boche, but none hit.

We arrived back at Captain's P.C. [command post] about noon and ate with him. Very nice food. Eggs, which some of the men had surcheyed, tomatoes, (fresh) stew, potatoes, syrup, toast and coffee. Bon, n'est-ce pas?

Altho we accomplished very little towards laying out any routes—we had had an interesting morning and some good experience—besides getting a good idea of ground over which we were to work for next few weeks and where we were to see our first American Drive.

We followed back along a ravine to Brigade Hqs. Had supper with the General again who treated us with the utmost deference.

Finis Part II

With lots of love and hopes that U all R in best of health; assuring
you that I am feeling wonderful—

*Je Suis, Ma Cheri,*
*Harv*

P. S. I decided this A.M. to grow a mustache—if the war lasts long enuf
I'll send you a photo.


*September 20, 1918*
*Somewhere in France*


Dear Pater,

I got your beaner of a letter last nite as I was starting out on an all night
job of loading our apparatus. Last nite was 2nd nite—tonite I know is
to be another. Hours or weather or sleep don't count in this business.

Dope has it we are moving to another stand—in other words we are
to become a travelling circus, no long monotonous stays in one area!
That'll be swell.

I am going to cable you tonite or tomorrow. My letters for a while
may be few and far between, but I kept notes of my experiences—you
may have received my first installment already—and as I get time
I'll continue narrating what I did. I think I was extremely fortunate
in having had opportunity to be in our first real drive and to have
been able to see everywhere—my passes allowing me to circulate freely
anywhere.

Re tank insignia. It's very Katish! I believe Bailey, Banks & Biddle,
Philadelphia [a jewelry store which sold military insignia] can send you
the designs. Try them.

Yes—the Tank Corps is absolutely independent—a distinct branch
just like Artillery, Infantry, etc., and believe me, boy, it's the nuts.

I have written you often that my work in Corps B4 coming to front
a month ago has been:

1 Month (in which I had to take course)

Rest of time instructor in Tank driving.

At front here I have been liaison officer with French Tanks, very interesting. My serial will go into it fully.

Don't let Mater worry! We didn't have a casualty in last show. Honest, we're getting by big—without any more danger than Q.M. Our tanks are small ones. They maneouver so wonderfully—they seem almost human.

Must close.

*Lots of love to all,*
*Harv*

*September 23, 1918*
*Somewhere Else in France*

MY DEAR ONES,
We just arrived here for our 2nd show to come off tout suite—talk about your travelling circuses—Richthofen's [Baron Manfred von Richthofen, so-called "Red Baron," a German aviator and ace.] was a pug along ours—2 in a week. But I can't give you any more dope now— you've probably received 2 of my serials by now. To think—20 pages and only thru first day. I've no time now to think it over but will get them to you as often as I can.

I couldn't get to writing this letter quick enuf. Just as impatient as a fellow to drive his new car. Why? Because out of a clear sky I got beaucoup from you all. Almost a month since I had the last and I'd given up any hope of getting any until I return to A.P.O. #714. Then to-nite after supper:

3 from Mater
3 from Pater
1 from Aunt Lettie
1 from Imy
1 from J. G. Stadilman
1 from Ruth Agar
1 from Rudy Matthews

O boy! I've stood corn woolley (canned corn beef) and coffee for almost a week—because rations couldn't get up to us on a/c moving up everything—artillery, etc. to back up our great success further south and to-nite to get the first fresh meat, potatoes, coffee, sugar, butter and even jam. And then that Mail. Ain't it a great and glorious feeling! Leave it to me to tell the world. That W.K. corn woolley will look like roast beef au jus, if I can look forward to another batch when this show is over.

I can see I take too much for granted even tho my verbosity, I know, would drive such good people as Pa Crowe or Miss O'Brien frantic. There are always points and thots that occur to me when I read your letters—that I want to clear up at once.

Hence this letter!

One at a time please! Let's see Mater's of Aug. 22nd.

Gee, I'd like to see Buns! Aunt Lettie writes that even while she was away Marilee seemed to grow taller. It won't be long. Next Spring—Boche finis! Pertat [peut-être] sooner. Then—the big permission! But right now we've got him on about his own 20 yard line with all his reserves in—and we with still the greatest fullback a playing—just talking to the ole man [coach Amos Alonzo Stagg]—and jumping around, warming up. Can you see that picture—on Stagg Field? He's going in after the next show. And when he do—wow!

Mater, you don't see Y a reject should get 4 bucks a day and a fighting man—only one? The fighting man ought to have to pay admission. He's seeing the show of his life. [Harris is referring to some then-popular song lyrics:

*Hip, Hip, I had a good job and I quit.*
*A dollar a day*
*Is damn good pay*
*For a guy that shovels shit!*]

I am certainly glad that you are so wrapt up in war work. It's fine and I feel sure you are not worrying about us. Don't do it. We're not taking a chance more than any of the other 2 million or so and the beauty of it is—we're getting fat on it. I really must get another suit of larger proportions as soon as I get back.

I have time and again tried to find some good Tank Insignia—but the frogs—our pet name for French—make 'em rotten.

I was going to order some for Imy and Ell. You write them and get their samples.

Let's see Sept. 7–5 days before our last show. I'll tell you where I was with a battalion up on the lines—slept in an infirmary the only place I could find a bed. Had four gas alarms—when of course we put our masks on—but the place was absolutely gas-proof.

And, Mater, I do hope you wouldn't read so much between the lines. In yours of Aug. 18th you say, "U were tired and homesick?" If a fellow didn't get homesick once in a while we would be in a bad way, I'll say. Why, honest, some times when it's quiet and there's nothing to do—I force homesickness on myself and think of what you are doing, etc., and it's a wonderful satisfaction.

You ask me about the temperature in a tank. Not so bad. Not much worse than in the front seat of a closed automobile. U.C. the fan sucks the air out of the compartment. We two stand into the engine compartment to cool the engine. We get air thru slits generously placed thru which we also see.

Why I'm just nuts about it—Jules Verne's *20,000 Leagues under the Sea* or Aviation are "as naught B4 us" as the good Einhorn's prayer book says. There'll be more romance connected with this service than—say— Horatio Alger could write about.

Why did I change? If you could see how those poor Ammunition Trainers have to work—as I have just recently! Never in daylight—always rain or no rain; over roads that eat your heart out if you have any feeling for the animals. Then when your old morale is lowest at 3 A.M. have a wagon get mired so that it looks impossible to extricate it. And all thru this the enemy is shelling your road. Pas bon! You can't fire back.

Of course Pater, had I known what I know now, I could very nicely have waited and then slipped over to the Tanks—with the captaincy. But c'est la guerre! I'll get it tout suite, anyway I hope.

Re your cables Pater, I received two I believe, but none via London. The one via Paris is much better. Now in reference to cables—I send them whenever I get a chance—and will keep you advised after a show— as soon as I can. But always remember—no word is as good as cable.

U ask if I am one of the "main guys" who shoot the gun. Oui, oui! During the other show tho I was with the French Big Tanks and we had trouble with the trenches so didn't see much action—but I've got a lot to write about that when I can sit down quietly—and it's getting late now. To-nite I am back with the A.P.O. #714 outfit for this show and will have something to rite you about that'll be good—I feel sure. I am not the driver—altho I certainly can make those damn little things maneouver so that they almost talk. Oh, he's a bear.

Reference that refugee child, I found he was turned over to the French Red Cross. Couldn't keep him. Aunt Lettie could write, say, to the American Red Cross, but the way these children are adopted is not actually being adopted. U just pay for their keep and the organization sends you pictures and keeps you advised monthly. Maybe apres la guerre you could actually get him.

Aunt Lettie—I received no candy as yet—next to a few more cigarettes (I'm rolling my own, now—out of Lucky Strikes) I'd like nothing better right now, that—with all this mail—and I'd be sitting Jake. But don't rush to send it—I'll be back to A.P.O.#714 B4 I could get it—and there—just as I packed them in the States, lie in beautiful rows—1500 cigarettes. Good place, n'est-ce pas?.

Well I must close now. U know that saying "it's a great life if U don't weaken"—I won't—but what I want to know is that you are not.

> *Beaucoup love,*
> *Harv*

*2 October 1918*
*Somewhere Else in France*
*Beautiful Sunshine*

MY DEAR ONES,
I certainly feel swell this morning—a wonderful sun—a universal itch and a day of rest. I hope to get this letter back to you thru some courier or otherwise. I've been so excitedly busy for the last six days since we went over for our second time that there hasn't been a chance to get word to you. Not even an opportunity to keep up my notes of the happenings, and there has been so much, too!

Yes, and since I started the above I've had a wonderful hot meal—one of the few in the last six days—made on a Boche field kitchen—and now I am smoking a cigar. Could anything be sweeter? I doubt it.

The doings here are about ten times as exciting as when we were in the St. Mihiel sector and I hope in 3 or 4 days we can get back and clean up.

U auto see my mustache—like a couple of old man Stagg's [Amos Alonzo Stagg, football coach at the University of Chicago] practice squads—11 prominent ones on a side and that's about all.

Saw a paper this morning and we are attacking from the North Sea to Switzerland, and Bulgaria has asked for an armistice. I guess old Fritz must feel himself slipping, eh? I tell the world that here, tho, we're fighting for every inch.

We're near the town that the French held so valiantly at the beginning of the war—and kept the Boche from Paris.

How are you all! I am hoping that some mail will come up for us tonite—then there would be nothing to it. But don't worry—and I have little doubt but that even B4 you get this letter you will have received a cable to effect that the shows are over and we're on our way to A.P.O. #714. That is if I can get to a telegraph office B4 I get back there.

I started out here with a haversack, the cane I found near Jaulny—in the other sector and a rain coat. The first nite I lost the rain coat and I'll be a son of a gun if it hasn't rained at least part of every day and most of the nites.

Altho it's impossible to take a bedding roll, pack some blankets wherever U go—unless you want to spend some damned cool nites—and oh boy, but the nites do get cold here this time of the year.

As soon as I had spent the first night it didn't take me long the next morning to surchey [chercher] a Boche blanket and overcoat and lo, when I returned to use it, some bum had hooked it from me.

Since then I've been living, i.e., sleeping and eating, on what I picked up. A battlefield an hour after we've advanced over it is a sight. No one need want for anything in way of equipment. Our boys might start off with the light packs but toute suite they drop everything but their guns. Well, imagine it and then when we arrive on Boche country. Beaucoup more! Dead Boche and much evidence of haste everywhere evident. Naturally many sights are pitiful—but c'est la guerre, and one has to get hardened to it.

I certainly hope you will keep any good hot dope in the newspaper since say the 12th of last month.

As I rote you I haven't seen or heard from Bud or Longstrethe but understand they are back at A.P.O. #714 with the new men that have arrived—probably same outfit Jack Agar is with.

For two days I have been acting in command of the company. Beaucoup Fun.

U should have seen me the other day. I no sooner walked into Division P.C. than a message came that the Boche were counter attacking. I was up there in liaison with the General awaiting his orders as to how best to use our tanks. When that message came it said Boche were already to a point 500 to 600 metres from us and coming quick.

The general ran out and said to get all men with guns up quick. I went along and ordered everyone up—some were resting, some walking around. One Co. of engineers were repairing a bridge, sent them up, and all the time Boche had a barrage.

Well, we got ready and then found it was all over.

Then the next day we had it again and I sent my outfit up and went up on foot swinging my cane—just like on Broadway.

When I got up there, about 3 km., I couldn't see either enemy or Boche. Nothing but Boche artillery firing at our tanks. Oh, it's great.

Kiss little Buns for me and with lots of love.

*Hurry for supper*
*reason for scribble*


*11 October 1918*
*In France*


MY DEAR ONES,

I am snatching an opportunity to drop you a line while I am here—and can get the letter off. I came out of the line the day before yesterday and am getting a little repos at Hqs. which is about 20 kilometers from the "show." I am in great shape, eating three squares a day here and I was even seduced into a little game of N.I.P. (national indoor pastime) and I did nip em, too, for about 1000 francs in a four hour session. With the same cards, Pater, you could have won all the francs in France. I had 20 franc notes piled up in front of me higher than American Family soap wrappers that I remember cutting out for Mater back in the 90's. I wanted continually to give them a chance and you know the old stuff—go in on a pair of deuces and draw two more and a Joker. And the beauty of it is that this is my second game in France.

Do you realize I have been over here 6 months! Old Syk and I landed at Bordeaux on April 12. Ça ne fait rien. Six months is considered from sailing date, March 29. As soon as I get back to civilization, which I admit will be entirely satisfactory for me, having been at it in the front lines since Aug. 25—I'll just slip the ole chevron on.

I have hopes of being relieved & getting a 24 or 48 hour leave & seeing Babe. After the session we have had they mite B a little lenient. In your letter you say his cable was marked "Nevers." I know it well. It's about 8 hours west of APO #714. Do you remember my first letter telling how we were stopped at a town at 12 o'clock at nite? After travelling 2 days and 2 nites with our men from Bordeaux & being advised that we were all wrong, that Coetquidon—just back the other way—was our destination? Well, Nevers was where we were stopped.

I received a letter of Sept. 14th from Babe. He seems very happy and satisfied. He just writes he received 10 letters in 2 days, "is fixed pretty—in charge of night mess crew—a good job—everything O.K. and prospects of promotion. They just made me private 1st class. There are rumors we are going to winter quarters in the Riviera. very monotonous existence but 100% better than infantry. I'm not kicking at all."

I always knew that he was pretty sensible—but he is more than that! That doughboy life is certainly a knockout and drag 'em out affair. The more one sees them, one realizes how wonderful and how hard a life they put in. It isn't the wonderful aviator or tanker that wins the war—it's the doughboy.

And, Oh boy! I think the greatest thing that can happen to a fellow is to get a bunch of mail before going over in an attack. Just to forget everything—gas up, oiling, plan of attack and the like—and sit down on a stump away from the bunch, lite up a cigarette and read the mail.

Twice now I have received 4 or 5 letters at a time just before leaving with our playthings. It just changes the whole situation.

I am glad that you have all the dope on the Renault and that it "all sounds like magic," as Mater rote. If I can just get some time off to write a few of the things that I have seen, without getting my English too complicated I am sure it will interest you.

It is a great satisfaction to have been actively engaged in the first two major operations of our army and our tank corps. I wouldn't have missed any of it for the world. But now that we are about due for withdrawal, maybe and perhaps, I am satisfied to withdraw.

Im writes the silk socks she is making are cootie-proof. What do you mean? Some cooties I have seen would require at least 1 sock to turn around in.

Just read Pres. Wilson's reply to the Boche request for armistice and if you were here you would know what General Pershing thinks of it. But remember when you read of our advances: they are slightly different from a jaunt down Mich. Boul. [Michigan Boulevard in Chicago] I haven't seen any hasty withdrawals in this section, except some I have made into shell holes when a M.G. or whizzy-banger opens up. Beaucoup!

Had the first bath in 2 months yesterday. In a nice white porcelain tub—tile floor, and heavy bath mat on floor. O oui! Like 'ell! In a large pot ordinarily used for making coffee. The shock of hot water was almost fatal. In fact any water, even on my face causes extreme agitation and squirming. 10 days—just over—and nary a wash.

Again I urge you not to worry. We'll be out in a few days and probably lay up all winter. And, hush! One of the K.P.'s (kitchen police who clean pans, etc.) told me confidentially that the general had told him that 50 officers were going back to the States, toute suite, as instructors. Now that's on the Q.T. Who can tell!

*Bushels of love,*
*Harve*

# 5

# REPRISE
# AND RETURN

TANK CORPS

TREAT EM' ROUGH

*A.P.O. #714*
*"Back Again Home"*
*About October 15, 1918*

MY DEAR ONES,

I sure am glad to get back and rest up a little—just sit around, write
some letters, go to the Y and hear some singing—other than Boche G. I.
cans [Heavy artillery]. Since August 25 up to the day before yesterday
I haven't been out of rifle range of our lines, except for a day or so every
couple of weeks. You have several of my letters from the St. Mihiel sector by this time? Then we went to the second show that our army put
on—in the Argonne. So that makes it pretty nice for me, n'est-ce pas?
First two shows that we as independents put on and first American
Tank units to get in action—and I there with both feet.

And here I am back on my birthday and with not a scratch or indentation of any kind—except from French itch, cooties, lice and other
animals. Funny thing—I didn't know I had the last mentioned playmates with me, until one made the mistake of coming out in the open,
and I said to a Lieut., "what in 'ell" just like that. He picked up said
beast and a mere cursory examination sufficed.

Honestly I didn't know I had anything but the French itch. I could
see it on my wrists. But there's the rub (joke). I didn't have the opportunity to take my clothes off since the first day. True, my body itched
all over, but "that must be the French itch," I mused. So I carried on
happily ignorant of other things, and it is a good thing I did. Not that
I could have done anything anyway. It isn't a nice feeling to know you
have bugs—so I was happier in not knowing.

And how thotful and good I was to them. Didn't bathe at all and
wore a nice fleece-lined woolen undershirt for the little dears to play in.
The only thing is that it wasn't fair to them—for me to let them stay
when a shell or bullet might have killed 10 or 20. That'd be cruelty to
animals!

And since I'm on this delicate subject: I got a letter from Imy today
enclosing some silk. It sounds "buggy" to me, but I'll try it. The idea is,
I suppose, to put it on socks, or sleeves to keep them from getting on
your body, & in that way, wear them out running up & down, trying to
escape & finally they die.

I just handed in a cable to HQs for a courier to take to town to send to you—to the effect that "Feeling fine—back to camp—not a scratch—Great birthday—love."

It seems as tho we don't connect very well as to exact meanings and thots to be read into cables, etc. "Back to camp" means back to APO #714. The rest is easy, isn't it? It's a great birthday—back after almost two months—worlds of experience—and now for a little rest in more desirable surroundings.

Pater wrote, "Why didn't you take Mr. Rosenwald over the ropes in a tank, yourself?" It isn't being done. That was a sergeant's job. It would not have been according to Hoyle. At the same time, mind ye, I had other tanks manoeuvering for the general.

That's great dope about Germany's possible evacuation. By the time you receive this letter it will be cinched one way or the other. Either it is another Boche game or La Guerre Finis! I suppose you will all be disappointed when you have to quit making bandages and selling war stamps. I feel the thing is going thru. I haven't any dope from HQs, and have no reason to divine from my recent experiences with the Boche that their resistance is weakening, if they want to hold—but I just feel that it's got to be.

I don't know where to begin. I've got so much that I consider of interest to you—that it is quite a problem. And it's dollars to doughnuts a lot of it gets boresome—But I must get it out of my system. Will continue later.

*Boku Love, Harve*

P. S. You auto see how I am fixed here. Officers remaining of two battalions who were up in shows in one barrack, not subdivided—no stoves—candles to write with—but with Buns' picture in two prominent places—All's well.

*October 18, 1918*

My Dear Ones,

I started a letter last nite but some playmates came in and started to hand out stories, "Remember the first morning we went over," and "that night in Death Valley when the Boche gassed us with everything they had" and so on. The stories are beginning to be built up. And, girls, they will be wonders in a few more narrations.

Sept. 6 was six days before we went over to St. Mihiel. Just about that nite I was up and out all nite waiting for the tanks to arrive—about 12 P.M., raining, and the darkest, coldest night I have seen for a long time. Out in the open, hiding in heavy underbrush to keep the wind off as much as possible. There we sat, the other Lt. who was working with me—"wondering why" and Lo! A flash lite approached closer. That in itself was wonderful enuf. It was a French Lt. and after flashing the lite in our faces, said in real England English, "You are with the tanks?" "Oui." "They are not coming tonite on account of a broken rail. But won't you come with me to my car and get warm? I am with the Railroad Artillery." Sweet Daddy! Will we? And we followed him.

Imagine our surprise on entering that car. It was about half as long as a standard diner, finished with oak or walnut panelling. A big table in the center with flowers in a vase. Beautiful hanging lamp equipped with electric lights. Pictures all around the room. Steam heated from the locomotive and like heaven to us, after a 6 hour wait, freezing.

We met his Company commander and 5 brother Lts.—the officers of that battery. They were sitting around a chess board, and soon as we came in, all came to stiff salute. No sooner done than this dapper little Lt. picked up a phone, called up the kitchen and ordered beer and sandwiches. Can U imagine it? Another went to a panel in the wall and pulled out a graphaphone [early phonograph]. With that combination it didn't take long to get clubby. Almost got to calling each other by first names. The standard joke was "trays beans." They couldn't get over that. Never did I taste better beer or fall into anything so welcome! For two years they had been together—at every front—from Italy to Flanders. We stayed several hours. Never ran into them again. From that place they were going to have no trouble laying 'em into Metz. So U can C they had some guns.

Don't you think that picture "Renforts à Oise" is great? I have thot of that central figure many times, up at the line. His expression, posture, I have seen it duplicated so many times. The same situation—waiting for the silent hand signal to go over the top—perhaps not to get more than a few feet before being shot down. And there they sit, waiting along the road or behind a crest. It all happens so quickly and you see this so often you are apt to pass by without a thot. But, gosh, it's made an impression on me that I'll never forget.

Mater, what do you mean we can't go on a spree when we get back? Them's hard words. Sanefarian, let's get back, then we'll see.

But talking about that let me tell you about last nite. I am now located about a kilometer from Bud in a big camp. Bud and Buddies have taken a liking to rum punch—rum and lemons heated. I slid over last nite and they were just beginning a brew. I left at 11 P.M, assisting a captain to his billet. And of all the awful walks, that one was a beaner. Time and again I thot I'd never make it. I just did. But dammit if I could get my clothes off. As a result there was no trouble dressing in the A.M.

If I see any cans labelled Swift's "corned-willy" I am going to send you a cable: "Sell Swifts." No interest of mine can make that stuff, if I know it. And yet how wonderful it tastes when you have been a couple of days with only a cracker and water and you find a pack along the road with a can of "willy!" Oh, boy, ain't it a great & glorious dish!

I am very glad, Mater, that you are interested in the tanks and are keeping interesting dope on them. At St. Mihiel I went over with a French outfit of St. Chaumonds. [Large, 25 ton French tanks, 28 feet

*"Teddy." The Renault St. Chaumond tank weighed 23 tons.*
*This particular model, shown here at Messy (Aisne), was driven by*
*French officers Socrate Bouillet and the future General Hitier.*
Photograph copyright Musée d'Histoire contemporaine (BDIC), Paris.

10 inches long, with 75 mm. cannon and 4 machine guns, and a crew of 9.]

I am acting company commander of C. Co. 345th Bn. and being a veteran now—the dope is I will keep this company and suppose get my captaincy some morning up at the lines, as several others have done. Promotion doesn't bother me in the least—from any angle I can handle it. The only reason it would be nice is this. Every day I hear of fellows back in the States, 2nd Lts. when I knew them—now Majors—and they have never been nearer the front than Healeys. Promotions over here are damned few and far between. Another point—people (who don't know, of course), will make me as dead from the neck up. 180 lbs. of bone and flesh and muscle: 178 lbs. bone above the neck and 2 lbs. of muscle.

Speaking of being a veteran. That's me. I wonder if you realize my situation. With the tanks in two shows and in both drives of ours as an independent army? I have just had transferred to my Co. some 90 men to bring it to strength. Yesterday I censored a few letters. I didn't have any insignia on—my old serge coat that never did fit and woolen breeches. Looked real hard! Several wrote "we are in a real outfit now. Our C.O. is a veteran."

Pater, Bud said, last nite, "Harve, whenever we get back I'm going to cable your Dad and have him meet us at the pier with boku beverages." "Pier, Hell," I says, "he'll meet us half-way." But seriously, there was some talk of officers going back but I am sure it's Bull. With Fritz moving all along we are going after him harder than ever—give him no breathing space until Wilson's demands are met. Don't make any plans to charter a boat, yet. Should such an eventuality come up, the cable wires will burn.

For a couple of weeks before Aug. 25 I was senior instructor which meant that I had 8 or 10 Lts. giving the enlisted men training in gunnery, etc. All I had to do was supervise it. I don't believe I'll instruct anymore, but will take C company up to the lines. There are boku new officers here and plenty for that work.

I have had some wonderful experiences. In my mind, the kind you read about. But not any more than any other Tanker has had. At St. Mihiel there wasn't much action. The Boche went too fast. Think of it. Our doughboys went 10 kms. the first morning. Our tanks had trouble the first day with the trenches. They were very wide and built on a poorly consolidated material that in rain changed into Mud. We had boku digging to do. I had my baptism of Boche artillery. It wrecked an ammunition train 100 meters away from me with about 4 shells. The method used by the Boche and by us of firing on trains and batteries is this. As soon as possible the artillery moves up after an attack to be most effective in helping the infantry. As soon as the doughboys move over ammunition and supply trains, artillery outfits start moving up to take up new positions. Boche planes come flying over and if near their own batteries they fire their machine guns in bursts of 5-10-15 or 20 shots frinstance—each burst being a signal prearranged which gives the range or location of targets. At the battery they get this signal and it takes about two minutes for shells to begin landing. Unless driven away by our planes, the Boche continue circling around, signalling for changes to make fire more effective. Each battery may have a plan attached to it for duty. If machine gun signalling isn't possible they fly back to the battery and drop messages.

When this Boche plane flew over this Ammunition Train it fired a signal and in 3 minutes the train was pretty well shot up. Horses, wagons and men laying all around. Something hit me a crack on the calf of leg. I looked down and found a piece of shell which had hit me. It was practically spent when it hit but it broke a button above my puttee. I jumped into a trench and waited until the shelling ceased.

A great sight is to get up on a hill or knoll and look back. As far as one can see the road is completely jammed with every conceivable moving thing. For miles! The nearest parallel that occurs to me is the way I imagine the Gold field rush would look like.

The night of Sept. 12 I slept in a Boche dugout that was the dirtiest place I ever saw. Dirty Boche clothes and equipment knee deep on the floor. From the window that night when we arrived at about 12 o'clock the whole sky was lighted in 8 or 10 places—where the Boche in retreat had set fire to towns they left.

Early the next morning we moved on to Thiaucourt, perhaps as large a town as we took. It was pretty well shot up—probably by our barrage. On the way we stopped 3 or 4 outfits were camped along the road, (I say "we"—French Capt., his Lt. and I). We wanted food, "Pas mange 2 jours." Finally we hit one kitchen and coffee was cooking. Ooo, la la! The French marveled at fact that up there under those conditions we had not only coffee but sugar and milk and boku!

The evening session has begun again. I don't know why but they all come in here and talk it over, Old Bunk and Bull stories. Going to quit for tonite. I'll drag these tales in now and then as I get a chance.

Just made up a package of souvenirs—2 Boche kepis- one enlisted man's and 1 sergeant's. The enlisted was a Bavarian I think from the printing inside. Also several belt buckles. I got 'em with revolver or machine gun. They stand for others I got whose kepis I didn't take. Doesn't "Gott mit Uns" get your goat? Poor deluded fools!

*Lots of love to all,*
*Harve*

*German soldier's belt buckle with "Gott mit uns" inscription.*
Photograph by Harvey H. Shapiro

*23 October 1918*
*A.P.O. 714*

DEAR FOLKS,
I haven't much to write. The longer I put off writing my experiences the less inclined I feel to tell them.

Mater, you ask why I don't write something about myself? Something personal. I can't grow a mustache for one. Pas possible! I have been twirling it and licking it with my tongue for 3 weeks. It can be seen, tho. You should have seen me in my fighting equipment. I salvaged (polite for hooked) a Boche cartridge arrangement—like a pair of suspenders (leather) for my revolver belt—to keep it from eating a hole in my hips. It worked fine. No insignia—lost it all. Steel helmet and French knife stuck in spiral puttee. Looked like a Senegalese or Apache.

I'm sitting pretty here, warm quarters. Best of all I still have all my equipment—bedroll, trunks, etc. All I lost up at the front was Pater's Gillette and an issue raincoat. I am way ahead on stuff I salvaged.

I have 2 bottles of rum cached which I take with me next time! As necessary as food when one is up all night and always cold. We are eating as well as at Fort Sheridan—as long as we are in camp—and except for days immediately after an attack. Here we have wonderful pancakes, big as a mess kit, creamery butter (canned in K.C.), syrup, jam, fresh white bread, meat, coffee, potatoes. Our Battalion (345th) considered as in the field, allows its officers to eat with companies. I prefer that to the officer's mess—which is rotten. Our ration now is $.42 a day. Imagine! The above food in correct combinations for 2 francs a day. Merveilleux! N'est-ce pas? Almost football training table rations.

At Thiaucourt I was with a French family who told some great stories. When we came there, they were in a daze. You could see happiness in their eyes, but otherwise, weary and worn. After some hours they began to realize what had happened and then you couldn't keep them from shaking hands and getting clubby. Time for bed.

*Lots of love,*
*Harve*


*APO #714*
*311th Tank Corps*
*25 October 1918*


MY DEAR ONES,
It seems to me that I have written a letter every day since we got back. I get a lot of pleasure from these little tête-à-têtes and I know you do also.

Before I forget I want you to know that this Tank Corps—without any "We treat 'em rough" or sign of the Black Cat slogan—that they have in the States is some organization—i.e., we original Tankers have already been cited TWICE. Once by General Pershing, himself, and by

General----who was in command of the 2nd show. Couched in wonderful terms they are conducive to increased chest measurements, to say the least. I am going to send you copies. Other organizations are in same orders of General----, but Gen. Pershing's is a personal letter to our commanding general.

All the above is just for effect and—while true—merely put in to lead you to the major point: I am included in a list submitted by my battalion Commander—"Deserving of special (something) for meritorious conduct" or words to that effect. Whether it goes to higher-ups I do not at present know—just in line of duty, that's all. If those above see fit something might come of it. This is for you alone, not for public or even family. I really would hate to have it get around at all unless officially. I thot you would be pleased to hear about it, for yourselves, remember! I am company commander, Co. C, 345th Bn., and as I have written you I seem to be in line for a "bump-up." When it comes—bon—if not, ditto.

It is very interesting to have 100 men for whom you are responsible and to whom they look for everything. Whatever. What you are the company will be. Quite a responsibility—but that doesn't bother me a bit.

Pater writes I had you all up in the air, like a minstrel, being a Tanker with artillery insignia & with a title of "Special Engineer." Tanker, I am—only insignia I could find was artillery in my rush to leave & called a Special Engineer so that no one wud know we were going to operate there.

These new officers haven't had quite enough "army" yet. They haven't the knack of getting stuff—unless issued to them. They haven't learned to whisper to the 1st sergeant, "Sgt, kind of cold last nite, only one stove in our room and U know, that's all they issue us, and as for wood 3 small pieces a day is all they allow us." Said 1st Sgt. doesn't even answer. He mite salute and say "Yessir" which means "I have you, Steven." Nobody knows what he does or worries either but toute suite—voila! Stove and wood. If investigated he mite have hooked it from the Colonel's quarters. That's how we get along and sit pretty so easily.

It's almost taps and I have to report to officer of day "all present" so will have to finis. I will be quite busy drilling and instructing company. Don't worry and imagine things, probably won't see any more action for months—just sit around, eating and sleeping and waiting for good weather in the spring when we can hit them as they never were before. Wasn't Pres. Wilson's note of Oct. 23 a hummer? No ambiguity!

*Love,*
*Harve*

*APO #714*
*November 1st, 1918*

My Dear Ones,
I had quite a set-back to note. For several days I have been expecting Knox Burns to arrive. Tonite his outfit arrived and I find he was detailed to stay in England. I imagine with Col. Hunter. Knox is going to get his captaincy toute suite, so a captain from there told me. That's fine. He auto. I also have heard that all artillery captains R going back to that branch. But c'est la Guerre. And Bud, Longstrethe and I remain as of "present grade." At times I get damn disgusted—not with myself of course—because I'm good but just with the way things have worked out as regards promotion. Pass it up to Tanks and then nothing. And the Joes in the States—2nd Lts. going to Majors for staying in the States.

To actually "take over" a battalion of Tanks and be in command of a company for a week up there—and then come back here and see these new outfits from the States captained by fellows who were drafted and made officers in one month training camp. Is all wrong! I am not the only one. All old tankers in the same boat. Something slipped somewhere. But I don't want you to get the idea that I am "low," I am not—just want to get it out of my system.

Look at the bright side! I have been up in the line for almost 2 months—in 2 big shows—with the fightingest branch in the service. In an outfit cited twice and still rearing to go. That's more than worth the difference. N'est-ce pas?

I am now with the 331st Bn. I was with 345th in the Argonne but returning here was transferred to Hqs. 331st—the idea being to scatter officers who have had experience among the new outfits. So far in ours I am the only one who has. The Adjutant told me last nite he had received a telegram from Major Whiting asking info. about me—that I was reported missing. I wired Lawrence this A.M., and also cabled you for fear I mite get in the papers. I put in my cable Nov. 3, "Well, Love." Missing, eh? The only thing I've missed is breakfast—when it was 90 to 10 in favor of bed.

I have ordered from Bailey, Banks & Biddle some insignia for you all and a paperweight in shape of a tank for Pater—for Xmas.

Understand Germany wants an armistice by noon tomorrow. Austria is finis. The only thing I want is a chance to play around on German territory. Then they can call it off. I really believe if we ever do we'll go as we never went before. Those damned Boche have it coming.

*So Long and lots of love,*
*Harve*

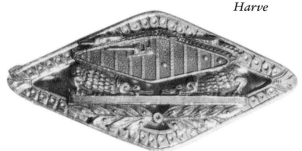

*Tank Corps collar insignia with gold tank,*
*silver dragons and laurel leaves.*
Photograph by Harvey H. Shapiro

*5 November 1918*

MY DEAR ONES,
I wish you could see my layout as I am writing to you. "Sitting Jake" couldn't cover it. It's more like "riding the gravy." Apres la guerre! And that doesn't seem so far off now with Austria's armistice already signed. Then remember, Mater, those Johnny Walkers under the front porch. Haven't had but one since I left New York and that was in Tours on my leave. Still "Old Robinson Rum" isn't so hard to take. I brot 2 bottles up with me in my bedroll. The only reason I brot anything intoxicating with me is that a British dr. said it would keep away the Flu and I believe it will! It has a double kick. Really peculiar. I advise "all

men who are fighting to make the world safe for the democrats," to leave home a pair of those wonderful home-knitted socks in which the heel bunches up about the ankles or sticks out above the shoetops—and substitute some of this. And made into a punch—one bottle of rum with a dash of water—it can't be beat! I know 'cause back at 714 Bud makes them regularly. His depiction of my attempting to negotiate the door is good. A tite rope walker or a burglar in the movies making his getaway! Honest that nite was awful. I felt fine, even stopped a couple of fites in the hut. "Absolutely all right." Then I said, "Guess I'll go out and get a look at the moon." It was about one km. to my quarters and I started there. At first I must have been making headway I distinctly remember the road moving. Then I have a recollection of great ambulatory effort. But the road or whatever I was on was 'standing still!' I don't know how long I was this way—but I do know my Boche cane never did a better service, even directing tanks, than that nite.

When I got in, a Lt. must have heard me—remarkable when I tried to be so quiet and he said, "I moved your cot against the wall." "Zat sho" and I sat down on the floor. . . The next morn I awoke—cane in hand and kepi tilted—otherwise ready for reveille.

The L of it is—that goes on every nite in Bud's place. We are going to set Bud up as a barkeep somewhere. He says he can stand anything but Pater's parties and cognac in his beer. He tells about that party you put on at the Brevort, Pater, whenever anyone will listen. He says, "Course I must have been drunk—as I have visions of people dancing on my face and a big brass flowerpot for a chin rest and they carried me away cold."

Sometimes I imagine I would talk for days on my experiences—then I can't think of a thing of importance.

But, let me tell you about my present quarters. It's in a town now absolutely in ruins except for a wall here and there- looks like a 240 G.I. can smashed every roof. They say Marie Antoinette was taken prisoner here [Varennes]. I don't know about that but beaucoup Boche were sent "the long route" from here a little over a month ago. I was here the day it happened, too. So returning has many remembrances. Up to 3 weeks ago it wasn't too healthy to live in any of the ruins either. The Boche built all their dwellings on the reverse side of a hill so allied shells couldn't get them. Now we have these quarters. It is reverting back to cliff dwelling with about 5 tiers of dugouts and lean-tos. Until our drive, the line was stationary for years so no expense was spared.

The rooms are wall-papered, electric lighted (we're still using their power plant), stoves in abundance.

In our room (I am with a 2nd Lt. who is Adjutant) we have a large wardrobe—as in your dressing room, Mater—except no mirror, marble-covered wash stand, and so it goes. If you think you need some little thing go out and "surchay" it. Anything one can desire is here in some dugout. The first day I came there were plenty of Boche rabbits in coops—ready to serve. I understand that tonite fires are to be seen near Sedan. They are still going back & burning as they go back.

Stuck into the wallpaper over my bed I only have 12 photos of Marilee and her large picture. That's the first thing I do—put up her pictures & then arrange my stuff accordingly. My toilet articles are neatly arranged on a small table. My clothes neatly hung in wardrobe. Hot fire in the stove. My striker is a wonder. U know what is a striker? Personal orderly. He put in a hitch or two in the navy so understands "cleanliness." I don't have to think about my personal stuff. My instructions to him were "If my stuff falls off the train your duty is to fall off with it." As a result I haven't lost a thing.

It is going to be very hard for me to get along without my valet after the war. Only one conclusion—Marilee must take up the job.

### THE WAR IS OVER! CAN THAT BE POSSIBLE?

In Wednesday paper Austria's signed armistice was published. Reports also showed Germans retreating along a 140 km. front. Today rumor kept coming in that Germany has signed her Finale. In army HQs. this afternoon the dope was insistent. About 20 minutes ago (8 P.M.) the damndest yelling began, not from a small group but simultaneously from different points. It sounded like 8 World Series games going on in every valley for miles around. Flares went up and every gun started firing. Right below me (I am in tier 4) a bunch of colored soldiers are singing *Swanee River*. It must be official! It's too big a climax to appreciate. It's become a business with me, I never think of civil life. It always seems so far in the future—something not to be counted on. And to think that all this is now, perhaps over! No matter what our thots, what must be the French and British feelings. Gee, I'd like to be in Paris tonite where some lucky birds are probably on leave or what's the matter with Chicago? We didn't get much chance up here to celebrate. Coffee coolers (swivel chair birds) have more opportunity. Of course I could finish my rum but—awful thot, what if it is only a latrine rumor and pas rum left. That would be a terrible situation.

I am sorry I wrote about report that I was "Missing." Sure as hell Mater will read between lines. I haven't had a chance to write Whiting yet. I did wire him, tho, denouncing it as an unqualified prevarication and nothing less than German propaganda to kill my chances at the polls.

I might have been missing from my command several times but I never missed an opportunity to crawl into a shell hole when 77's or machine guns played too strong. My record to date is three hours in one hole. What a beautiful hole that was—the kind one can stand up in—symmetrical sides, about half as big as our room. I am going to perpetuate a fund to keep that hole in perpetual bloom.

It was the day we went over with the 1st division. I was acting Battalion Commander. We had gotten thru a barrage of 240's with only a few casualties. A lot of my tanks were scattered from hell to breakfast and I went on with a couple of runners, hiding now and then behind a few blades of grass as machine guns opened up on us. I didn't know where our infantry was. I was too busy ducking to notice. Just then a machine gun opened on us. I looked back and both my runners had been hit and were being carried back. I couldn't make out where that gun was— so I started crawling—and ping, ping, ping. I lay still—just barely creeping, my steel helmet pushed along in front.

This kept on for 100 meters and I slid into this grand oasis of a hole—taking a final glimpse around with nothing to be seen. I watched for a tank but none came. Trying to dope out where the firing was from I put my helmet up on my cane. Ping, ping, ping. That bird thinks he knows me. I waited, trying his aim at intervals until finally I figured out I must be ahead of the infantry. As long as I stayed there I was OK. I proceeded to munch some German hard bread. At about 2 P.M. when I couldn't get any metallic response to my cane—helmet I got a little brazen and crawled over the lip of the hole. Still nothing! In an hour or so I was among friends. Our infantry was digging in about 200 meters back of where I was. Do you wonder why I feel so well disposed toward that shell-hole? One of our tanks afterwards put 4 Boche out for the count in that same nest.

Now I have staff job again: Supply officer for the 331st Bn. 3rd Brigade, Tank Corps. My days of excitement are over—if there is a general armistice. As S.O. I don't get near the fighting at all—just work from the railhead up—drawing equipment & supplies. The same job I had with the Ammunition Train for awhile—remember? I am not a glutton. I had a couple of months of the real thing—and there are so many who are raring to go.

But it is wonderfully exciting. There is nothing to compare with an army attack—the preparation—H-hour, it's more than exhilarating. One can't get the same feelings from anything else. If the Boche put up a strong resistance—as they did here—one just has to go about his work—because if you worry about his counter-barrage getting you, you'll get worn out. And withal, it is just a business.

I can hear your remarks, "Why does he get changed around so much?" Here's the story. We went back from here to APO 714 after the 2 attacks when I was Co. Commander. We were back a week during which we were reorganized and re-equipped. Then one of the old Captains, who did not get up in either show, and who is Bn. C. O. for one of the new battalions from the states, asked that I be assigned to his outfit. I, being an upright young man, 26 years of age, not often kissed and having had experience at the Front. None else in his battalion had.

So I went over and told him I would take his damned supply officer job, temporarily only. So I got assigned. It's important work—that food, oil, gas & ammunition get up when needed. When an attack is imminent it's all done at night. The roads near the Front on a night preceeding an attack are unimaginable. Can you imagine 800 to 1000 big trucks, artillery, staff cars, Fords etc. going up and a similar line coming back over a road just wide enuf for two vehicles to pass—a road always muddy and skiddy? One truck break-down and there is hell to pay. All this time not a light—not even a match is struck. One can't help but marvel at the truck drivers. It's uncanny the way they can get thru. They go ballin' the jack 15-20 m.p.h. when it's impossible to see the radiator.

We were only back there for about 10 days, then returned by train. The line has moved way up. We couldn't get up in 2 days—and from reports—never will catch up with the Boche dragging out the way they are.

Tonite (the 3rd nite I've put in writing this letter) I understand that the Boche are conferring with Marshal Foch. When you get this letter the thing will have been settled.

Did you ever stop to think what this war is going to do? Make old women out of us! See some street car conductor who happened to be in the same show as you—and the street car company will get a couple extra fares out of you while you talk it all over again. Or I can imagine a situation where you might bum a guy for a cup of coffee or a schooner by mentioning some mystic word like St. Mihiel, Vaquois or the like. Trays beans!

I am going over in the old sector—one of the large cities to see about getting some tools, etc. It's a long auto trip so will have to leave early. Hence Good Nite.

*Love,*
*Harve*

*November 11, 1918*
*331 Bn. 3rd Brig. T.C.*

DEAR ELL,
With armistice on there's nothing much to do—so we just eat regularly (I'll bet any meal wud be a banquet at your place), sleep well and let Uncle Sam do the worrying.

This afternoon I went "salvaging" which in the A.E.F. is equivalent to a picnic in the States. It consists in going over Boche layouts, dugouts of all kinds for souvenirs. It's lots of fun. Some places you go into might have been a German Major's, frinstance. They mite have allayed toute suite or be still there lying in a more or less uncomfortable place on the floor. Everything else intact. Bon! He mite even have an Iron Cross or a gold helmet. All of which immediately changes hands—without argument.

I had a lot of stuff—pistols, field glasses, etc.—but all has been lost or swiped! So now I've got to go out and try and get some more.

But it's hard picking. Everything good has been hooked. I only got a French and Boche helmet—a Boche suit of armor—which some of their machine gunners wear—and some shell cases—today. Don't think I'll worry much about trying to get it home. I sent some kepis and belt buckles—with "Gott mit Uns" [God is With Us] on them home about 3 weeks ago. Also have some more of those and some anti-tank bullets in my trunk at A.P.O. 714. Maybe I'll C that again.

Every cap represents 10 Boche, that's just approximate.

What gets my goat tho is that beaucoup officers who never saw any action are buying up these souvenirs and will have great stories to tell apres la guerre.

I have had a lot of great experiences—shooting Boche and jumping into shell holes when shot at. I've been very fortunate—when fellows like Bud Fisher and any number of others—never got near it. Feel sorry for them.

I came into this town we're in now about 6 weeks ago in a tank. The Boche had machine guns in second story windows, and when they didn't bother us they'd throw hand grenades on our tanks. A couple of 37 mm's most often sufficed. Any of them in the streets would run like wild.

By the time U get this U'll know more than I about the peace proposition and how it's working out. No one knows how long we'll be here—but I would like to see the Rhine and be in that army of occupation for a while!

I got that candy from Fields' [from the London office of the Marshall Fields department store] that Mater sent and I'm eating it very sparingly. It's great: 1 can of Toffee, ditto hard candy, 1/2 lb chocolate, lemon drops. Just the thing.

It'll be Christmas toute suite—my 2nd away from home. Best of luck and—Y say—your birthday is in Dec. aussi! When I get back—we'll take in a movie—Big time!

> Lots of love,
> Harv

*November 13, 1918*
*331 Bn. 3rd Brig. T.C.*

DEAR PATER,

La guerre es finis. U no doubt knew it B4 we did, altho we had rumors for several days—and say, it's a wonder the Boche can keep the river that runs right under their bridges. Pretty stiff terms for an armistice, 's what I mean! The only thing I regret is that we don't get a chance to shoot up the Fatherland. I hope the Tanks will be a part of the army of occupation. I could pick out a good billet in Cologne, frinstance. But I don't C how we can be used. Therefore we mite be among the first to go back.

[Answering a question of his father about battlefield salvaging, Harris writes:]

Everything is salvaged by a regular salvage outfit, just as soon as shelling ceases & is sent back (this includes brass cartridges, guns, wagons, etc.) to army salvage dumps. What can be—is reissued. The balance is made over, or scrapped. I don't know what happens then. But it is surprising how soon after the action things are cleaned up. Take the place we are now in, for example. We took this town Sept. 26th about 3 in the afternoon. After that for 10 days or so the going was damned slow, but then—Oh la la! As a result by the 1st of November the salvaging outfit had been through & you can't see a piece of equipment.

I have picked up all kinds of Boche souvenirs, but lost most of them when tanks I'd thrown the stuff on got hit or lost. The doughboy is the souvenir getter. While they're advancing in an attack they frisk a Boche for the pistol or cross, or under shell fire they investigage dugouts. It's lots of fun. I suppose at that, tho, the guy from the S.O.S. will buy more souvenirs & have wilder stories than anyone else.

Season's greetings & love to all.


*November 17, 1918*
*Apres la Guerre*
*In France*


DEAR LITTLE BUNS [Harris's little sister, Marilee]:
Today is your Birthday. I bet you are having a great time. No School! because it's Sunday and I suppose you are not glad, eh?. You are 6 years old. Just wait until I get home. You will get beaucoup patches. No monkeying with me as you do with Imy. Francis and I will both know how to talk French and we will talk to Mater and Imy in French, and you and your big sister, "ahnorie" [Eleanor] won't know what we are talking about.

It will be almost Christmas when you get this letter. Just wait and see what I am sending you. I hope you get lots of presents. Now Kiddie, be a good girl and don't study too hard. Do what Mama tells you or look out when we get home.

Bon jour, ma petite, comment vous portez-vous? Je suis trays beans. Et vous? Avez-vous vin blanc? Non, non, Je desire le rum. Beaucoup Zigzag, tout le jour. Pas bon française, n'est-ce pas? Au revoir, ma Cherie.

[Part of the same letter was addressed to his Aunt Annie. Answering her questions, he wrote:]

You suggested we should take a nice trip over Europe oo la la! I may care to return say in 1930 or so, but now? Retournez toute suite, sufficient pour moi. I would like to go to London for a day or so, but I'd just as leave get a little better acquainted around Chicago:

> To see the river striving to flow for all the load it carries,
> To sleep in a bed—not a Boche's bunk
> And take a look around all of Harris' junk.

But them's my sediments.

Do U know what I'm going to do for a month straight? Take in three musical comedies a day and hear every Victor record ever made. Am absolutely famished for music.

*Lots of love*


*November 24, 1918*
*Varennes, France*


DEAR DAD,
This is the day put aside by our old friend *"The Stars and Stripes"* for the writing of "Dad's Xmas letter." The Ed. knows damned well that the old Gent hasn't come in for much—and it is a pretty clever stunt! Guerre Finis—son may soon be back looking for a job and bunk and an occasional touch.

The same paper advises that censorship is off on letters. It's the first time I have put the name of my station on the letter, and except for a couple of slips, perhaps, I haven't mentioned any names. I certainly wanted to mention names plenty of times.

Since I have been here my itinerary has taken me over a considerable part of France. From Bordeaux and the rest camp there we loaded with our 196 men to meet and join the 3rd Ammunition Train. After 2 days we heard we were going to Chateau-Villane (not far from Chaumont). 3rd Division Hqs. was there. We came thru Angers, Angoulême, Bourges,

Tours & at Nevers we were stopped at midnite. Our destination should have been Coetquidon, but where in hell was that? Couldn't find out. Finally going back over same route we got to Ploermel in Brittany near Guer. No trains out that day or until next morning. So we went up to the French mayor of Cantonment, told him our story: 3 days and 3 nites on train (40 men to the car), 3 days rations all gone with another day still to go. We wanted to billet our men in beds ce soir. Oui. Oui. [The remainder of this story is contained in Harris's letter of April 13, 1918.] Finally arrived at Coetquidon. I wrote about trip to St. Nazaire and Rennes—but this stuff is tiresome.

You ask if I got a shot at any Boche or took any prisoners? A few. Couldn't get some. At times they were all around, ready for the picking. I shouldn't wonder but that my total would be large. There were times when it was impossible to see results on account of the warmth of the situation.

I'll tell you of one instance that gave me more satisfaction than

*Visibility for the Renault tank driver was very limited during combat, when the front doors were closed. The driver, shown here, sat beneath his crewman, the gunner, who stood. In the photograph French Alpine troops stand near the Renault tank.* Photograph copyright Musée de l'Armée, Paris.

I can describe. With one tank which I was in, we were going up a small valley. The doughboys were in skirmish formation and we were getting hell from a machine gun that was shooting 100 a minute easily. It's hard to see out of a tank—let alone a camouflaged machine gun. All I could see was doughboys getting bumped off—most of them on the ground. As I approached the gun was turned on the tank and I could see figures in a bush 10 feet or so up the bank. At about 50 yards I gave them a 37 shrapnel—but they kept on shooting. At 25 yds. the gun was stopped (I was headed right for it). Then the usual thing happened—universal Boche trick, except for Prussians—those 3 Boche came out with their hands up. I was sore. They certainly gave our doughboys a chance—like 'ell! They came a little toward me. Paying particular attention to best way to get all three I put a H.E. [High explosive shell] on the ground between them. Those 37 H.E. are small but they did the work. That afternoon those 3 Boche were still there, i.e., within a radius of 30 yards. I never felt more satisfied at anything. U asked what kind of tank I handled. I had a Renault Mosquito tank. That day I had a sergeant driver—altho a corporal usually does drive.

And do U know that if they have to cover an open area with 2—3 or 4 guns they all don't open up on first target that appears. Each has its own field or sector actually laid out at the gun with tape along the ground. Each fires only at objects appearing in its own sector.

In the Argonne it was all "over the sights" direct fire with artillery on us, from hills, etc. Imagine a battery firing at you like so many rifles. Tres interessant. It's unfortunate if a shell goes thru the tank and explodes (some 200 37's) but the occupants never know it. One case where this happened, the driver didn't get a scratch, but the gunner was unrecognizable. But withal, it's a sport par excellence. Have a lot more stories, some even more dramatic. I'll guarantee to keep you interested as long as you can keep me "numb"—boku zigzag.

*Harv*

P. S. Don't give these stories out. They'll put me down as a b.s. artist and besides pas bon.

Have boku souvenirs. If I can get them home: German helmets, French helmets, 3 or 4 guns, Machine guns, shells, caps, a Boche citation card, etc. etc.

*December 1, 1918 — Sunday*
*Varennes, France*

AT ROYAL POKER CLUB
[The name given to the unit P.C. or Poste de commande.]

DEAR ONES,
Just finished a roast beef-mashed potato dinner which was trays beans and waiting for the members of the R.P.C. to come in and report. We have a bell rigged up and a code to warn us of approach of suspicious characters. 24 hours to play, no excuses, and no questions asked. The R.P.C. is in the third tier up from the road, a brick structure, & consists of two rooms. One occupied by several Lts.—the other a reception and gambling room. On the walls are pictures of wonderful movie girls. We spend nearly all of our time here not necessarily gambling. Our club room! We borrowed a mandolin and Norton from Minneapolis is playing it. In addition good cigars and a warm fire. Voila!

Talking about a fire—it's just crisp enuf to need one—sun, frosty A.M. and peppy days. I wonder where we would be now if the Boche hadn't quit. They sure as 'ell would have had boku fun. Great weather for tanks—a whole lot better than we had when we were going over regularly.

An indication of how the Boche officers lived here: a stone building devoted to shower baths—2 real bathtubs (first I have seen in France). Our battalion barber shop is located in a room rigged up for a drinking room—like a cove in a salon of a ship—subdued green wallpaper— heavy plush seats etc., I suppose all the stuff was salvaged from French homes rite here.

But talking of shower baths, there is an interesting site below us now. 400 Boche prisoners (from a nearby cage) are here for their weekly bath. A motley crowd. I was talking to the Lt. who has charge of them. Their ration is better than ours, by orders. If they have any complaints they can write to G.H.Q. Candy is a regular issue. Many of them used to bathe here once a month. Now they have to every week—which detracts from their other advantages.

I had an interesting A.M.—paying the Battalion. I wrote about putting in the payrolls yesterday. This A.M. I paid it out. Came out to the centime.

If you have a topographical map look up the hill about 200 meters west of Clermont. We unloaded from the railroad there and laid up for 5 days nestled safe back of that hill. The Boche knew we were there, saw us unload and they shelled the hill continuously but couldn't get us. The shells hit the top, or went way over. We just sat and laughed at them.

At D-1 day at 8 P.M—the darkest night I can remember for some time, we started for the woods. It took me about 4 hours to get my tanks there. Darkness and continual truck trains—fan belts breaking, clutches sticking, and every once in a while running into gas (poison). As we got up close we couldn't even use a flash so we guided the tank drivers by walking ahead smoking cigarettes by the package. Every one doing his work regardless of what was happening. A shell comes over close and all fall into ditch at edge of road, and bound up again like a football player who throws himself at some interference and lands on his feet. Then it's quiet and we go on. At Neuvilly the Boche were shelling the Bridge. We got over O.K., but it got some dough-boys. A few groans—and we went on. Not what we thought, but it was nothing out of the ordinary. The mind works peculiarly. The Boche were shelling and gassing. A captain had a detachment of men in the

*A Renault tank being transported by railroad.*
*This was the preferred way to move fleets of tanks from sector to sector.*
Photograph copyright Musée de l'Armée, Paris.

town and asked me the route to somewhere. I didn't know but I stopped, got behind a wall, looked at my map and figured out his route. In the meanwhile my tanks got a couple of hundred yards ahead. My point is all circumstances are common place—everything moves normally. If it didn't there would be no organization. From Neuvilly on the doughboys were moving up in columns of twos—then supply wagons, kitchens, etc. "Fall out" would be given and they would slump down in the dark at the edge of the road making some remarks as tanks went by. I had seen troops moving up the night B4 the attack and always have the same feelings. A lot of them will get bumped off tomorrow. I have seen articles that in true American style they sang . . . No such thing. We all have the same thots and it's hard to write them.

"We'll lay in behind the first woods on rite after Neuvilly." No chance to see the woods. Too dark. The men, walking along the same road appear like a moving black wall, 6 feet high. A flare, a couple of kms. away shows the woods. Some of the other tanks are already there. I found a place for mine. They mite just as well have stood out in an open field—because we leave before it's light.

From Corps orders some of us knew that the heavies would open up at 1:30 o'clock (H-4). When they start at 1:30, the 75's and light guns will open up. That means two hours of intense fire. We leave here at 4 A.M. Can get near 4 hours of sleep. No cover of any kind—no coat—just a haversack with me. A cold rain is starting. Before the crews turn in there will be a final fill-up with gas and water ( a dump was started that evening). Reserve gas not to be used but will be carried. Stamping around for the softest grass there is nothing to do but try to get some sleep. The men are O.K. as they have their blankets. And it's darn cold and wet, too. It isn't policy to get near the woods on account of gas in it.

There she goes! Here's a chance to set your watch. The heavies open up at 1:30 and that doesn't mean 1:30 and a half. The booms are heavy and deep, on our right and left. None close, but every time one goes it lights up the sky like a blast furnace. It isn't very intensive. I'll bet the 75's at 3:30 A.M. will wake Fritz up to the fact that something is coming off. I squirm around and get a little comfortable. And why "I am a son of a gun," I must have slept 2 hours! It's almost 3:30 A.M. One hour more and we leave here. Two more and we go over.

Then a bolt seemed to hit us between the eyes and jar us against the tanks. I'll bet that battery isn't over fifty feet away. The flame from the guns show the crews working like a movie. If you think such a situation isn't stirring! Marvelous. That battery must be the one we passed on the road. Hell! That isn't the same one as before. Must be two of them darned near hub to hub. Can that be a third? Why, that damn field is full of them! And they are firing at will. Certainly giving the Boche hell! Another St. Mihiel. It's wonderful how the organization works. "System" is an army invention. Everything on the dot and millons of men to handle. No use trying to sleep so lite up a cigarette, pull yourself in, snail-like, to get as warm as possible and watch the show. What if my tank should "die" with a machine-gun playing on it? Turn the turret around and get out on the other side. There mite be a chance to put it out of action first, tho. Suppose the M.G. on my tank jams with the hand extractor lost somewhere en route. 7 hours difference in time makes it about 9 o'clock at home and they are probably playing solitaire. Some man nearby thinks he is at home, snoring to beat hell. Then the hollow noise as the back compartment of some tank is opened up. Time to get up and go. "Your tackling was rotten. U played like a jackass." Then the timekeeper sticks his head in. "3 minutes more," he says. Between the halves has similar feelings to our leaving our final "laying up" place. In no time everyone is stirring. The fun begins. In 40 minutes we'll be over! Do you wonder why, now, as I ride back 10 to 15 kms. and pass that woods, I do a lot of thinking? And some lucky ones may be home for Xmas.

My R.P.C. playmates are calling.

Lots of love and greetings to all,

*Harve*


*No Date*


The editor has received numerous requests from his readers in Poughkeepsie, Mpls, Chicago, New York, etc., for a continuation of his narrative of St. Mihiel. The Argonne was a "show." St. Mihiel was a rehearsal. More of interest happened in Argonne in 5 minutes than at St. Mihiel in a day. Besides I have notes on the latter. There was not time at the Argonne. Realizing that he is a bear at quantity—but lacks quality—he has decided to put in one or two bits in every letter.

## AMERICAN ARTILLERY DESTROYS BOCHE BATTERY
Thanks to tank officer there are a few more good Germans.
They are DEAD!

Every time I look out of my window I see a ridge which is the old valley walls of the insignificant Aire River. It's about 400 meters from Varennes, and by looking more determinedly I can see the very place our tanks laid under its protection. We were there for 2 nites, Sept. 27 and 28. On the morning of the 29th with the 35th division having awfully hard going south and southwest of Charpentry we were ordered up to assist. I had been up most of the nite before and felt pretty rotten. At 4 A.M. we started to get ready. Our Mess sergeant ____ (Do you remember I wrote you from Chickamauga how a sergeant of mine got an awful beating at the Chattanooga Athletic Club at a prize fite?) Well, this mess sergeant in Supply Train (the guy who done it) was up at I A.M. Water for coffee had to be carried from the foot of the bridge here at Varennes. At 6 A.M. we had coffee in the rain and dark. I felt better, and was too busy looking after the tanks of my platoon to do much damning of the Boche for making us get into the war. Just before leaving a Lt. stuck a bottle of something at me—"Boche cognac"—Bien, and I felt "trays beanser."

At about 200 meters from the juncture of the national highway (road we were on splitting—one way to Charpentry, the other to Exermont) I could see that the Boche were shelling the junction with G.I. cans [Shells loaded with high explosives and bits of wire and scrap metal]. A captain, whom I knew was on the staff of 35th division, stopped me and said, "Thank God! We can't advance on account of machine guns." It wouldn't have made any difference to him if the opposition was 420's. He'd have wanted our little tanks to clean them out, anyway. It's surprising what they ask us to do. Doughboys to Generals have sent us against places a battleship couldn't capture, but that is outside of the story. "There are snipers along the road, U'd better get in your tank," he cautioned. I walked a little farther and saw two doughboys go down—then decided to get aboard. It isn't an easy matter for me to get into the tank thru the two small rear doors even when in training—let alone with haversack, pistol, etc. I was hung up for a while—but got in and lumbered down the road. There didn't seem to be anything going on so I climbed out and sat just back of the turret. My feet hanging inside and my body protected in front of the turret.

I passed the General [Brigadier General Samuel Rockenbach] and his staff, sitting in a gully at the side of the road. I'll never forget the expression and the appreciative, "You are just the man we are waiting for" as I rode by. This look did more to thrill me than words could have possibly done.

And still nothing stirring. As we approached this juncture, tho, things began warming up. The Boche were no more than 500 meters away with their 77's and 88's—and they knew the importance of shelling roads! I was jarred a couple of times from concussion of exploding shells. Then I noticed my C. O. (Commanding Officer) at side of road—I spoke above of General and staff in a gully 3 feet deep. When one speaks of a General's post command (headquarters) he imagines the "old man" in a bomb-proof shelter, orderlies running around, telephones ringing, and the fight miles up ahead. Not so in this war! I haven't seen a brigade yet, but what the general was up in front and his post command wherever he happened to be: along the road or in a shell hole. I have seen a general at Apremont as soon as the tanks got there and ten minutes before the infantry arrived.

My C.O. motioned for me to pull my tanks over behind a hedge which I did; and camouflaged them as best I could. But they had been heard rumbling along. It would be luck if we weren't hit. But they weren't—altho whizz-bangs—[A flat trajectory shot from a 3 inch cannon]—( the kind you don't hear until they hit) came all around the tanks all afternoon—until the batteries that were firing had to withdraw. With artillery hidden and firing at your tanks the only thing to do is hide yourself and them.

After the tanks were camouflaged I went to Capt. and several Lts. in a gully nearby. This gully ran out into Aire Valley. After we settled down I decided to see what I could by going to the edge of gully and looking across Aire Valley about 1500 meters.

There I was, safe from every shell and looking out across to flats on other side of river, where two companies of tanks (our two battalions) were advancing in line, infantry following at several hundred meters. Just as pretty as the show we had put on at Bourg for staff officers [probably referring to a demonstration held for staff officers of IV Corps on September 19-20, 1918]. At far edge of flats was the east edge of Argonne. Everything seemed to be going well until a shell exploded amidst the infantry. Then another in front of the advancing tanks. Then another to the right. The doughboys immediately flopped down and the tanks continued, not knowing it. Then I saw a puff of smoke where the forest jutted towards me and a shell exploded within ten feet of a tank. Several turned for a depression near river—the others went for the woods, not knowing where the shots were coming from. And there I was, unable to do a thing, probably the only one who knew where those guns were. The flash had told me and with the aid of glasses I could actually see the Boche gun crews working, loading. If my voice would have carried I could have yelled, but that was the instant the #1 (man who fires the piece) had his hand on grip and was going to fire. That was out of the question. I thot of firing with a 37 mm. from a tank but probably wouldn't get within hundreds of yards. The range was about 1000 meters. Too much for a 37.

What to do? It was getting late. In half an hour it would be dark. The doughboys, I could faintly make out, were digging in. The tanks were in the woods and might at any moment come directly in front of the battery. For by this time I had been able to make out at least three guns. Something had to be done damned quick!

I looked around and a Capt. and two enlisted men were approaching my point of vantage—which was a darned good one for an observation point. The men carried wire and field phones. As the Captain came nearer I saw his crossed cannons and before I could say a word he

*Three Renault tanks parked in the village of Neuilly St. Front (Aisne).*
Photograph copyright Musée d'Histoire Contemporaine (BDIC), Paris.

said, "I am going to set up a forward P.C. here. My battery is back there a ways. See anything to shoot at?" "Well, I'll be damned," was all I could say and pointed across the valley. What had sent him here at that moment? Three minutes later I would have gone back to where I had left the Capt. and he would not have seen the battery as it was fast getting dark.

I "came out of it" in a fraction of a second and told him the whole story. Meanwhile he had ordered a phone rigged up from the battery. While waiting for this connection he set up his telescope and figured out his data, etc. "Hurry, hurry in ten minutes we won't be able to see a thing 100 yards away," I thot to myself.

"Hello, yes, this is Capt _____. Is Lt _____ there? Take this data—Work fast—Range 2200 H.E. sweeping." Four reports whistled over us. Four flashes. I estimated a couple hundred yards short of target. "2600!" He kicked up the range 400. They were lost in the woods. "They ought to be worried now," he said. The deflection was OK, three rounds, "on second piece close 5," and 12 of them went over us, and eight at least landed right at that corner of woods. "That's got 'em!" I saw two guns get direct hits. The crews must be finished, too. "You have done something today, Capt." I said. "Wasn't that fine?" he answered. And it got dark so that we could hardly see valley directly below us.

I went back to tanks and found that a runner had been looking for me for an hour. The tanks had already gone back behind the hill towards Varennes. What a different nite I spent to the preceeding two! It was still cold, wet, & raining, but I was warm within. "Tomorrow I'll show him that observation tower near Apremont. Some more good fun," I thot as I sat on the running board of our Mack truck (the inside and underneath were crowded with enlisted men) and went to sleep as best I could.


Thursday A.M.

Just imagine writing my personal experiences—in 1000 words—100,000, maybe—yes! [See the Appendix.] I'd just finished enclosed letter and narrative to you. So am sending that in as an experience. This might be better but too much to rite one.

*Harvey*

*Tuesday—Dec. 10, 1918*

Dear Folks,

With a graphaphone that someone salvaged playing *Silver Threads Among the Gold*, *Perfect Day*, *Mother MacCree* and similar heart pulling pieces, I can't refrain from writing home. Every other nite we've played cards but to-nite, everyone is writing. What is it in music that does that? My thots have been everywhere, but come back to "what are the folks doing to-nite"—and to the last time I heard music that made a lasting impression on me.

It was a km. or so from here, in a valley between Charpentry and Baulny—on Oct. 3. We've called it "Death Valley" because of the hell we got there continually day and nite. But on that nite for a change, not a shell came over. About 10 o'clock the truck came up with mail. Beaucoup excitement. The war was forgotten! Then we thot of the Boche piano we'd salvaged. One of the Lts. has a wonderful tenor, and he sang wonderfully—the same pieces we're playing to-nite. Picture it! Just his voice, and no other sound-with light accompaniment. I'll wager there wasn't a man but was around that piano—with thots you can well imagine. There wasn't a day since we first went over here that we hadn't had casualties, and a lot of their buddies had been bumped off. While Doug was singing a courier arrived; the 35th Division was being relieved and we were going over at 5:30 with the 1st Bn! Now we'll go! After planning and disposing of different things that had to be done—we turned in for a couple of hours—under a sheet iron roof we had improvised. Capt. English and Lt. Llewelyn [Matt English and Robert C. Llewelyn]—both killed the next morning—were the most optimistic. They'd made a reconnaissance that afternoon. Bob had been my bunkie for three or four days and was always pulling something humorous, such as ordering a taxi in writing on a field message blank—and sending it to someone by orderly; or ducking when a shell came over and remarking "I'm not scared, just cautious, that's all." (The general of T.C. is reported, alleged to and said to have said he was going to send 50 officers back to the States as instructors. Bob said only, "Who are the other 49?") I hardly saw him the next morning in the "Getaway." It was the darkness just B4 the dawn and every crew was tuning up motors waiting for the barrage to open up so that the racket the tanks made moving (imagine 50 of them) wouldn't give the whole thing away. At about 10 A.M. Capt.

English's orderly and runner came up to me with the news that Capt. English has been killed a few minutes before, walking ahead & tending to his tanks, and that Bob's tank had been hit by a 77 which set off some 200–37's in the racks of his tank. That was enuf! I don't wonder that the only thing found was the identification tag on his wrist. Out of about 15 officers that went out that morning 4 of us came back. Two killed, the rest all wounded. Do you wonder why such music sort of "gets" me even tho the war is finis and there's nothing to look forward to now, but work and pleasure?

As long as I have the necessary "Inspiration" for writing which I haven't had for some time I mite as well take you thru that day—Oct. 4th. Some day of experience! Our jumping off point was 4 or 500 metres up on a plateau about 50 ft. above the valley we were in. When the artillery opened up at about 5:20 we started out. It wud only take us 10 minutes to get there with the infantry. As we went up the hill it grew lighter and I distinguished the support infantry in shallow trenches standing at their machine guns putting over a machine gun barrage. Also every gun shooting at will and as fast as the belts could be put in. As we went on it was evident we were late. The infantry had already gone over and were on their way, and the Boche counter-barrage had opened up. There was nothing to do but speed up and go into line (from column as fast as possible) so U can get a picture of it quickly— in column tanks follow at 10 to 20 meter distance and when line signal is given the tanks fan out from fighting formation, and if we go over with a Battalion the 50 meter interval would be cut down—if with a regiment—increased. In other words we have to cover as much front as unit we are attached to. As soon as a platoon (5) tanks came up over hill it opened out immediately and the Lt. in charge led direction as arranged the nite before. I was company commander and when tanks had opened up I had my first opportunity to take in the situation. For the time being the platoon commanders had their orders; to proceed in advance of infantry, cleaning up machine guns or anything else that might hold up the infantry. Here's the reason for high standard even among enlisted men of Tank Corps; 4 or 5 tanks in platoon are commanded by sergeants, and when a man gets into a tank, I don't care if he's a general, he can control his tank only—especially under stress of battle. No signals yet conceived have worked. Every tank is independent except of course for the larger ideas as to what objectives each must strive for—in which case every one had definite orders. That's why I impress the men often with fact that they are not tank sergeants—but commanders. Before they go into a show they will get all instructions and information we can give—after that—it's up to them with the exception that a Co. C.O. has 3 or 4 runners with him for purpose of carrying messages to platoon or tank commanders—with instructions as the events of moments necessitate. Often—if possible, Tank Co. C.O. goes with Inf. Bn. Commander, who is constantly getting word by runner and otherwise just what situation is everywhere.

Well, for the moment the platoon commanders, 3 of them, would be on their own, so I looked around a little. The barrage of the Boche grew heavier as soon as the tanks came up over the hill and my first distraction from checking up to C that my 15 tanks were all there still, and going bien—was that I almost tripped over a doughboy lying on the ground "Gee, he got it quick," I thot. I didn't know if he was killed or not, but said "Where R. U. hit, buddie?" His head was face downward in the ground. He turned his head a little looked up and said , "My leg, will you turn my ankle a little, sir?" Then I looked at his leg, and one foot was lying over the other—but at an unnatural angle. Then I noticed blood all over his legs from thighs down. I lifted his leg as gently as I could and put it the way I thot it ought to be. He winced. "Most likely broken above the knee but the stretcher bearers will be here in a few minutes. U'll be all right." "Thank you sir," he said and I ducked on.

I've never seen a more terrible, yet wonderful counter- barrage than the Boche laid down on us as we advanced that morning. Not 77's but 105's and 240's and just as regular as could be; as we advanced the range was dropped and the shells fell always rite in our line. It's wonderful to think about afterwards but hell to go thru. Well here's what U have: infantry and tanks advancing in line and shells falling at rate of 20 or 30 a minute all around you. I'll bet I spent half that morning falling desperately and without any mental restraint; then jumping up, only to go down again.

I kept my tank about 50 metres behind me, and my three runners at about 20 metres. That's along same line I spoke of above—one can't control more than one tank—in a tank—so we walked ahead or with them.

Now and then I'd make some changes, order up reserve tanks to take places of tanks disabled or put out of action—and in the first 20 minutes or so about 5 tanks were hit by direct fire.

Then the platoons scattered for their different objectives or to help out infantry held up somewhere. I was beginning to lose touch with the tanks, altho I could see them scattered on both sides—some stationary and probably firing on some M.G.; others out of action with crews crawling out to make hasty repairs or walking back to later lead a repair man up to it; others still—doors closed. Direct hit and both of crew bumped off? Perhaps one or two at uncomfortable angles in holes—stuck—they'll sure as hell get hit toute suite if they stay there!

Just then an infantry Lt. came up—evidently noticed red, yellow and blue brassard on my arm and pointed out a clump of bushes. "Boche M.G. nest there holding us up," he said. I looked over. There was so damned much shooting, explosions and noise that I could hardly hear him—let alone hear that M.G.—but I did notice our doughboys 100 metres or so from there—on their bellies and crawling along. Then one or two stopped crawling, finished! I motioned back to my runners—for one to come up. I noticed there were only two. When the one came up I asked him first, "where is Smith?" "Dunno sir, but I believe he went back, little too much for him!" "Well, I'll be damned! Go over and have Sergeant so-and-so take his tank up to that woods, M.G. there." I never mentioned a thing to that lad later for running away under fire. Damned serious offense—but I could notice he felt it.

I couldn't help but watch that little redheaded kid as he went over with my message. Any picture you have ever seen of message runner, ducking—could beat it. Draw on your imagination! He had guts! There the little tank stopped, he delivered his message and the tank just followed along parallel to clump of woods, layed in four or five 37's. The Sgt. in tank opened up rear door, motioned to the doughboys- and another nice gain was made, and in this way we went on until 10 o'clock or so. By this time, tho, I lost communication with all my tanks—had even put my tank in a platoon to replace another. Here, on the one side of them mite be down a small valley, and I was unable to see them, and elsewhere woods intervened.

All this time, mind you, I was in and out of shell holes and most of them just made. Some big enuf to put our room at home in—just sort of hugging the sides. If possible the safest place to jump is into a shell hole just made as it is not likely that another shell will end in same place. The biggest danger is not from direct hits by artillery, (I have seen them tho) because that one can't prevent and when it happens the objects hit—never know it. There can't be any pain! The mean part of it is fragments. Pieces from a pencil breadth to a jagged 4 or 5 inch piece. They are always whistling over you. When a shell hits and explodes, the pieces go out into a cone shape as far as 200 yards, from explosion, so that theoretically if a man could stand at X and not die from concussion—no fragment would hit him. With shrapnel it is different. These are fired—not to explode on impact but the fragments are coming down on you. With high explosive the thing to do is get something (bank, etc.) between you and point shell is going to land. With shrapnel, theoretically, a man standing upright is exposing a minimum number of square inches to the fragments and what you need here is overhead cover.

I said above "where shell is going to land" which would seem as tho you could tell. After a while one almost can tell from noise shell makes as it approaches. I remember in Death Valley we used to sit and call them "over"—"short"—"400 metres." "Close, duck!" Exhilarating! How do you tell? Blow thru your teeth and hold same note and steady volume of air. That's going over and won't bother you.

Now blow and make above note slowly changing to whistle doing down the scale and growing louder—then a "boom." That's closer but not dangerous.

Now omit above note and have just the whistle with a "boom." I've been flat on the ground for 3 seconds—waiting for you to get out that "boom." Tres pres!

Then, and I believe the worst, is the Boche 88 (really the Austrian 88) It's just a "whizz-bang"—no whistling, no noise. Lands and explodes before you've heard it at all.

In some places I found myself behind front line as it advances—in others (one of which I'll describe in "very" great detail) ahead of it. Machine gun companies—37 mm. field batteries (same gun practically as we use on our tanks)—Colonels with their runners—prisoners coming back carrying their own or our wounded—a whistle signal here or there for a platoon to get up and start going—and then—a burst of 3 or 4 shrapnel and a couple of high explosives (as some Boche batteries got the range accurately) and not a person standing or thing moving. No sooner over, but all jump up again and move on until the next valley.

It was during one of these lulls that a Tank Lt. with me now, got a glimpse of one of our tank commanders—a sergeant—coming back. Gosh, but he was ashen white. Especially against black leather football-helmet-like helmet we wore in tanks, which he was wearing. The Lt. went over to C what ailed him. Here's the story: This Sgt. was gunner with a corporal driving. They were going thru some heavy brush when he felt the tank sinking away from him. They went down for, what he imagined, 15 ft. or more; and when slipping the tank was turning on its side. Then water began pouring in the slits. The driver couldn't open his front doors—due to weight of water or mud—and when they realized they were turned over and submerged the driver said: "We both can't make it. U get out!" The Sgt. managed to open the back door and got out. The driver was drowned! Then, no sooner out, but our dough-boys thinking him a Boche began firing on him. Nothing could be done and another chapter of heroism was finished—one that will probably never be known.

By this time we approached down the valley S.W. of Exermont. The sides go up 40-50 ft. In bottom of valley, still smoldering, was an American flying machine—all wrecked and crumpled up. We looked for the aviator and thru the wreckage and smoke were just able to distinguish a form in sitting posture shrivelled up beyond recognition—charred, black. He had probably fallen only a short time before.

But I'd seen so much death and wounds that morning! Still I'll always remember that L shaped figure, shrivelled and charred—the machine still burning.

We started up the sides of the valley—when Pinnng Pinnng—Pinnng—and we were all out flat on the ground. That S. of a G. is close and thinks he has our number. We all thot walking into a machine gun nest is not so bad—but to be stalked by a sniper when you can't tell where he is—is another matter. There were no other troops around—but our party. It's a cinch he'll get us in time.

All we could do is lie perfectly still for when we did he didn't shoot. But where in 'ell was it coming from? We started crawling and I happened to look back and saw the bullets hitting the ground on other side of valley—kicking up little clouds of dust. An imaginary line from those points—over us—is direction shots are coming from.

By crawling up the slope we could get under a ledge and there—safe—mite be able to see the bugger. We accomplished this and by this time could dope out pretty well that he must have been up in a tree—a

little back from the edge of vallley. As we went up the slope and got
under protection of ledge he couldn't get us. From under ledge by skill-
ful observation we picked out where he was but all we had were revolvers and the range was couple of hundred yards. Every 30 seconds or
so a shell came over and landed in valley or on opposite side.

After deciding to work around him and get closer and just ready to
start—a tank came up, Voila! After giving crew instructions, we waited.
Heard a couple 37's and the tank came back. We could go on now. And
we did. Besides the sniper's post in there, there were 2 M. G. nests along
back of valley and at each gun—3 dead Boche—in all positions. Some
"opened up" by direct hits—others just dead. All good Germans (dead).
At each nest was an anti-tank gun—just a big 7 ft. Mauser rifle.

But the tanks were to rally at Exermont in the afternoon—and we
had to get there about 1000 yds. away. From here on things got much
more intrikate.

We weren't accomplishing a damned thing but, I'll admit, were having a hell of a good time. What we had to do was collect as many tanks
as possible and reorganize.

Sitting in shell hole, I sent word back by runner to the P. C. as to our
locations and what situation looked like, etc. Then started on. We were
getting into a hot bed ahead. Careful listening told us there were at
least 3 M. G.'s ahead somewhere. We probably wouldn't have gone
ahead if we stopped to think. It's best not to, often. And soon we were
out—on an open plain and we were in it. A temporary lull and was now
becoming a mad house. Possibly 200 shots a minute were being fired—
perhaps all at us. We hadn't noticed any other troops for half an hour.
Down on our bellies—we'll make it by jumps from shell hole to shell
hole.

Did you ever think how awkward it is to be lying out on a flat land
with bullets whistling over you and suck yourself in all you could-
pushing your helmet ahead of you—with your nose—still feel that
nothing can avail? If I can only make it behind those 4 tall pieces of
grass or behind that lip of a shell hole! Even that wagon-rut would be
something to sidle into! And a shell hole 6 inches deep! That would
be merveilleux. That's how naked and uncovered I feel. One of my runners had been hit and was lying on his side and another one, the little
red head, was on his side at arms length, applying first aid. Thing were
looking a Leetle bad for us. The field was several miles square—not a

tank, a few doughboys and us—with Maxims furnishing all the entertainment. There was a slight rise of ground 20 yds. ahead of us and a ring of loose earth. It's our only chance—if it's a decent sized shell hole! If it wasn't we'd be more of a target than ever—sort of on a rim of a crest.

We played and won! Never have I seen a more beautiful sight—the 7 wonders of the world not excepted—and some day I'm going to lay aside a fund to keep it perpetually in bloom. One by one we went over into it—head first in seal fashion and there was still room for more. Its sides were as smooth as if done by hand; and 8 ft. deep. Just think of the comfort of standing up! Nor did we get in without being observed. Tout suite, G.I. cans came over, and those W.I. fragments whined over us. Nothing but a direct hit would bother us now.

But weren't we in a pretty predicament, tho? Shells landing beyond us and all around—and 2 maybe more M.G.'s to keep us down and the latter proceeded to do that! I stuck my head up just once, sufficient! About 20 shots came at me in a fraction of a second, hitting up dirt, grass and small stones. That wasn't healthy! "You can see what chance we have of getting out," one man said. I stuck my helmet up on my cane—Pings beaucoup. Nothing to do—but sit "pretty." Every 15 or 20 minutes I duplicated my cane trick, with the same results. I had some Boche hardtack in my haversack (about size of sugar cubes—sweetened a little and quite good) so we proceeded to eat some.

Unless they come out after us—we only had 4 revolvers—and could certainly get them as long as our ammunition lasted, we would have to wait until dark to make our getaway. We next saw a Lt. and two enlisted men crawling nearby and yelled for them to come in. They made it amid another volley. He was scout officer for 26th. Inf. (1st Div.) and was trying to find out where the 18th Inf. was. "Where is our line now?" I asked him. "About 500 metres back there." He pointed in direction we'd come from. No wonder we were being so royally treated with M.G. and Boche artillery. Our front line was ½ km. back and there was nothing else to attract their attention at that time.

After 2 hrs. and 45 minutes of this—during which we studied maps, wrote a field message—to be sent back at first opportunity advising need for reserve tanks and unhealthy status of Exermont, I succeeded in cutting a groove in dirt as in direction of M.G. Probably see something now. But not a thing. The next time I put my helmet up—got no response so we decided to try and duck back, by making an awful quick rush of it and falling as soon as the M.G.'s opened up. Just a chance that we'd all get by unhit.

But not a shot came, if any did the wind was whistling by too fast for us to hear. I'll bet my haversack (wt. 25 lbs.) stood out straight.

But we made it to cover, sent report back and were eating cold beans and hardtack when we heard of Capt. English's and Bob's deaths. Am going to Langres, will continue later.

Love—

*Harvey*

*Varennes, France*
*Wednesday, December 18, 1918*

DEAR FOLKS,

Gosh, but it is disagreeable out today: raining, cold and beaucoup mud, but within it's trays beans. I have had a 3 day trip to Bourg. I went with Lt. Norton—in a Dodge—last Friday noon. In nice weather the ride is enjoyable, but to me, of late, riding around France has become very tiresome. Have seen enough of French towns, people and customs. Ballin' the Jack [a railroad term meaning going very fast], we make it to Langres in about 6 hours—thru Bar-le-Duc, St. Dizier, Joinville and Chaumont.

What did I go down for? Just to see some of the "old timers" at Bourg. Knox is there now. When I got in Friday nite I walked into Bud's hut. He was in bed and was surprised, but also sort of expected me because he'd written me a couple days B4 that he was going on leave the 15th (which letter I haven't yet received) and he thot I'd come down to go with him. He was going the next morning (Saturday). He put in for Nantes, Lyon & Nice (sort of exceptional request to put in for 3 places)—and he got it. He borrowed 800 francs from me so with what he had he auto have a bon permission. Of course he was going to Paris first.

That nite Norton and I—aided by my perfect French—found beds in a French poilu's home. Hotels are all crowded.

Saturday morning I looked up Knox and Longstrethe. The latter, especially, is "nuts" about going A.W.O.L. if necessary to come here. "You are my last hope of seeing the Front," Longstrethe says. "You've got to arrange it." Maybe I cud arrange for them to come up on mail truck but the latest dope is we are leaving here (Varennes) for some billeting area in 1st army region back around Bar-sur-Aube or St. Dizier. This Bn. for instance will be billeted in a small town. The other Bn., this Brigade, the 345th, in another town nearby. But just where, I don't know.

Knox is a Captain and Brigade S.O. He looks fine, but is pretty peeved at not getting into any action—and I don't blame him. I was lucky as I am the only one of the 3rd. Ammunition Train who transferred to the tanks to get into it. To my mind that's worth more than half a dozen additional bars.

Did I ever write and tell you what Capt. Compton—Bn. C. O. of Bn. [Ranulf Compton] I was with during the show—told me? Now this is just entre nous. "I have recommended you for your fine work to the Generals, Colonels Patton and Pullen—[Daniel D. Pullen, Chief of Staff to General Rockenbach] and for promotion. Capt. Combs has asked me to transfer you to his Bn. and I am doing that but I hate to lose you."

The recommendation for fine work, etc., mite have been bunk but the promotion part went thru, I understand—but the armistice killed it. Since then a general order put a stop to promotions. Another week and I would have been "kicked up." The only thing I look for now is "out" instead of "up"!

I bot a pair of white Bedford breeches. OO, la, la,—A Paris tailor has a representative at Hotel. They'll make a hit for dress. Also I bot some Q.M. serge from Bud for a suit and am having that made,—first clothes I have bot since commissioned. You can imagine how my whipcord blouse looks. I wore it from Aug. 25 to Oct. 15 practically 24 hours a day, slept in it. The suit will be done in a week or so.

Sunday A.M. after using Bud's bunk, I ate at the officers' mess at Old Center. (The new Tankers are at the New Center.) And it was like old times—when we were a big family. A lot of the old officers are going back to the States with a "surgeon's certificate of discharge" from wounds, etc.—not because they are maimed or in bad shape—but because they can put it across and get home. Others are with different outfits.

Lt. Burgess (I was with him all the time at St. Mihiel) and I had quite a session reminiscing. Then we got a hunch to slip down to Dijon—which is supposed to be a 2nd Paris. It's about 60 km. from Bourg. Our orders were only good to Bourg from Varennes and "the M.P.'s are pretty strict," some officers told us. So we went on assumption that no one would know where Varennes was & we'd just tell them we were on our way back. Look at the map—just in the opposite direction, but sanefarien ["It doesn't matter."]—and we got by with it, too.

Had a very nice dinner there & bummed the streets and cafes until 8 P.M., then tore back. It is a conventional French city & that's all I can say for it. The only good feature was that I bot a bottle of scotch at the Cafe Chateaubriand. Absolutely the first I have been able to get anywhere. It must have been a bad day for the fillies, tho—as there wasn't a good one to look at but stay away from—woman on the streets. Everybody else was out walking. Crowds everywhere.

Monday A.M. went to Langres to finish shopping. I had a "try-on," bot a comb and brush, Eau de Cologne and cognac. Went to see Cap't Palmer (Rudy's father-in-law). Rick (Rudy's brother) was killed. He and four others went out and 5 Boche planes appeared below them. From the little I know about it this is a good situation—merely dive down on them. But 5 more Boche appeared from above; and 3 or 4 of our planes went down—Rick's among them.

I certainly am content that I could do my bit in a branch such as the tanks—otherwise it would be depressing to have such men die while I played a safe game. This is personal. I wouldn't want Babe to have an idea that I think that way of him and scores of others.

The trip back Monday was in rain all the way and you should have seen our car—big packing cases on running boards—one pair of 11EE shoes (one man can't wear anything smaller) hanging from the top; a lantern, 10 suits of baby soft pajamas (from Capt. Palmer) and 5 cases of cognac.

It is very likely I'll go back there shortly with a truck & get fitted out with Red X socks, sweaters, etc. for the men.

And a week from today is Xmas! Wouldn't it be merveilleux to be home! But no chance. And yet every now and then in the papers Gen. March [General Peyton March] is quoted as saying that Tank corps will get home at once. It is evident we are leaving here soon. Not later than the first of the year. We have to move from here because everything is leaving. We are practically the only outfit in this region. The other nite coming home from Bar-le-Duc we didn't pass a conveyance of any kind up to Varennes. How times have changed. 45 days ago it would have been impossible to pass.

This noon one of the Lts. brot 2 English women, nurses, in for lunch. They were spending their 3-day leave bumming around over the Argonne, getting rides on trucks, etc. They have been nursing since 1914—have been with the British in Egypt and are now attached to the French. Both past middle-age, and one was from Montreal. Quite interesting. Both were of nice, pleasant feelings toward the Boche. It did me good to hear them. One with a medium touch of Irish said she wished she had the guarding of prisoners. "I'd ride a motorcycle and make them keep up with me. Any that wouldn't would be shot" was her plan. Notwithstanding the terrible treatment our men got and especially the British, we treat the damn Boche with kid gloves: shower baths, warm clothing, no work in the rain, regular candy issue, and invited to make complaints. They are not worth it. These nurses told us of men released by the Boche without food and walking 100–200 miles to Nancy—no clothing, emaciated and sick—many arrived only to die in the streets in front of the Red X. It is such stuff that makes us hope that something still will prevent peace and we can go into Germany, and for a day fall as low as the Kultured Boche did for 4 years. If we could I'd wager we would do a more thoro job than they did. With a just pretext to go in and kill them! I'm getting rabid, maybe—but I believe not. And then Boche women writing French mothers asking for leniency, white bread and help. I can't go on.

I can't imagine the celebration over the armistice. I experienced none of it and as far as any different feeling is concerned we have none of that, except when we hear of some outfit going home. Then we are pinched into the fact that the war is over. I left Nancy the Sunday before armistice was signed, got back here and it was Wednesday before it came out in the papers. We were about ready to leave here and go up into action near Sedan. So the only difference as far as we were concerned was that we stayed here and every doughboy shot off and up every gun or flare he could find—besides if there were 5,000 troops in valley nearby there were 5,000 bonfires.

Nancy, during the war, was the darkest city in France on account of air raids. Everyone carried a flashlite and U'd be walking along—pitch black—and a flash would come in your face. As a result the "filles" would have a lot of fun. We knew there were bon cafes there—were directed to the very doorways & entrances & I'll be damned if we could find places to go in.

You mention in your letter that Levin was mentioned as a casualty avec portrait in newspaper. He couldn't even get a good drunk. I met him at Dijon. Tell his mother to ease her mind, he's alrite unless a truck hits him.

The reason why I didn't send a Xmas box coupon is that none were issued to our outfit. Anyway I couldn't think of a thing that I need—except some photos. I have boku candy, cigars, a locker of liquor, cigarettes—and this afternoon, another bath in our Boche bath house in a real porcelain tub, filled to the brim with hot water. Could anything be sweeter?

I have a helmet I am going to mail, and besides a box the size of a locker trunk and another half again larger—filled with everything from a Boche water-cooled Maxim M.G. to a Boche bugle. In my trunk at Bourg R buckles and antitank bullets (latter very scarce). I only hope I can get them home. Among them are shell cases from 37 mm. to six inches—good for hatpin holders to umbrella stands.

In connection with anything Boche I might mention that I am also in possession of an unknown number of fleas—two of which I know from scouting parties, wear two service chevrons each. If I can catch them they will be listed as "killed in action." And last nite I awakened out of a good sleep, and saw Lt. Cunningham who bunks with me—looking across the room towards me. "What goes on," quoth I. "I was watching a rat running over you and on the box over there (souvenir box is at my head). I have put some cheese on the floor and wonder if he will come and eat it." Nice quiet entertainment!

Mater, there is no worry about my becoming a "regular," altho in your letter you don't specify "regular" what—officer of the regular army or a regular drunk. A list came around a week or so ago getting officers' ideas:

   A.  Regular Army
   B.  Immediate discharge with reappointment in Reserve
   C.  Immediate and absolute discharge

We call the last "immediate divorce and no alimony."
I put in for "B."

*January 2, 1919*
*Varennes*

MY DEAR ONES,

The next morning (after a dance at a new Red Cross club in Souilly) being a working day I was awakened by an orderly at 9 o'clock who had a telephone message for me. A deuced hour, don't you know? It read "Lt. Matthews will call Lt. Harris at 9:30 from Verdun." I dressed tout suite & after waiting around for a couple of hours finally connected with him. He was there but was leaving in the morning to look up Rick's grave. Transportation is getting very difficult especially on non-official business. Time was when I could get it. Now it is tres difficile. Finally all I could get was a sidecar [motorcycle with attached seat]— with right rear fender missing & raining like 'ell. They make a wonderful bath tub. B4 the Armistice the roads were kept up in wonderful shape, now they are terrible. First the sparkplug got a short, then the brake wouldn't work, then something else & all the time a perfect stream of mud came back at me. I was a wreck. But even that wouldn't be so bad, but it was pitch dark when I got to Verdun & no lites. I was to meet him at the St. Nicholas Hospital. No one knew where it was. The streets are so eccentric, concentric, that even if the Boche got into the town I'll bet they couldn't get out. Finally I called up the Graves Registration Bureau & told men to send a man down to get me. Rudy came instead. His operation doesn't bother him, but, of course, Rick's death was a blow. He always worried about that.

We found a bed in a French officer's room there & sat around the stove talking French with 2 Captains until they turned in. Then we continued until about 3 o'clock smoking our heads off & discussing everything from religion to cognac.

I came back the next morning about noon. Rudy was up against it for transportation but finally was promised a sidecar by the C.O. of Base Hospital 15. He was going first to Fontaine, then Don-sur-Meuse. I hope he has been successful but he doesn't know within 30 km where Rick fell. A Captain who was on same expedition (& they started out Sept. 26 to bomb in daylite) & who was about the only one to get back was able to give Rudy only very meagre information. He believes Rick was shot down about the same time he was. The Captain—later in a Boche hospital—was shown Rick's identification book. So there is little doubt but that he was killed. But the Graves R. B. [Graves Registration Bureau] hasn't got up there yet & imagine trying to find a grave between Chicago & Highland Park. They had accomplished their mission & had swung around to the rite when attacked from above. I certainly hope he finds the grave. He certainly would but his time is limited.

After I left Rudy at Verdun I rode back in my portable bathtub in a driving sleet-like rain. Terrible. My impressions of Verdun? Very much different than I'd imagined it. I thot it a hillside just ploughed up with shells, nothing standing. Forts a total ruin, etc. When I saw the town the next morning I was never more surprised. Every fifth or sixth house a wreck, that's true, but I've seen few towns anywhere as near front as Verdun was that weren't wrecked a whole lot more. Why Varennes here with only a few walls standing (one store front with "Pharmacie" on it, another "Mairie") [town hall] is a real wrecked town. Verdun, altho much smaller reminded me of Nancy which was never shot up, but bombed pretty regularly.

There are no civilians in Verdun. I didn't see the Forts which were taken—all but one—by the Boche (the town itself—the citadel—never was). I knew full well tho if I had a frog go over the ground with me & explain the situation it would have been very interesting. I noticed particularly a large cathedral, from a block or two away it looked like the Madeleine in Paris & it didn't seem to have a hit. They say that underground there are provisions in way of billets, dugouts, etc., for 30–40,000 people.

Sunday A.M. I took a Lt. to a hospital near Fleury. He was badly burned, due to a little friendly Boche trick. We were salvaging artillery with our tanks, pulling the guns out of their position and it was cold as L and rainy. He went into a dugout, saw a stove either filled with wood or else he put some in and lit it. A lot of gun cotton was mixed with the wood and Blooey! Damned lucky he is alive.

Ruth and a Miss Taylor came back with us. Our dinner was rotten—no potatoes, no milk, no butter, etc. We are the only troops up here and no one thot about giving us a full ration. The colonel is taking the matter up.

After dinner, at 3 P.M. or so we went up on the hill to give the girls a ride in a tank. Lt. Tenny and I tried to start about 8 tanks, primed every one, cranked and pulled and worked. At last one went. Just the same as when we were in action. Like any motor you are lucky if you can get them started in time to jump off. Well, finally, when almost dark we took them for a ride, in the tank and on top of it. It was a mean day so we all went down to the P. C. and talked until supper & shortly after went back to Souilly. Lt. Norton (from Mpls.) went with me & after eating some homemade doughnuts—chocolate, etc. returned.

It was fine to have them here. The whole bunch sat with open mouths, in silent admiration one mite say—to be able to talk to real American girls. 2 or 3 months of crude living and careless language makes bums out of most of us.

Lots of love,

*Harve*

*Chalons sur Marne*
*24 December 1918*
*Day Before Christmas*

DEAR FOLKS,

Tomorrow will be my second Christmas away from home—and from arrangements we're making for food and wines it should be quite a day of feasting and good cheer—Altho not even a good alternative for home.

During the last week the only thot of our command from Colonel down, it seems, has been to skirmish around and purchase things: Beer at St. Menehould; turkeys somewhere else; wine, sherry; "erfs" (oeufs) here at Chalons, and so on. Nor R we the only ones at it—officers are going every where with trucks surchaying stuff. We bot turkeys yesterday for 12 Fr a kilo—that's about 5 francs a pound. Is that too much? We could get geese for a little over 3 francs a pound. Damn those francs—one spends twice as much as figured on, due to constantly neglecting to figure out, "how much is that in real money?"

I came down here yesterday in our Dodge with Capt. Combs (Bn C.O.) and Lt. Tenney—from Decatur. From Varennes, this means going thru Argonne. A very interesting trip! One marvels at thot of French and our being able to "clean" it out. It is a beautiful, hilly forest similar to—Imagine! the Tennessee Mountains.

On the way down we stopped at a little town about 10 kilometers from Chalons and went into a Cathedral there. The first time I've ever thot of "inspecting" as we used to in '06. It was begun in 750 or so by Charlemagne, in commemoration of his father Charles Martel. I do not think it has any particular other points of interest. I didn't see any.

But let me tell you what we are going to have tomorrow! Turkey—par cranberry sauce; mashed potatoes—vegetable soup—peas and corn for vegetables—chocolate cake. Then wines and liquors, assorted kinds,—avec le toute also 2 barrels of beer.

I do not know yet if we are going back tonite. Capt. Combs went back in car last nite—so we have to take train for St. Menehould where car will meet us. I know this tho—if I don't get back I'm going to have ham and eggs tomorrow for breakfast if I've got to cook it myself. Then we'll allay back.

*January 26, 1919*
*Bourg, France*

Dear Ones,

I'd about given up hopes of getting any more mail in the AEF as I supposed U'd be expecting me about 1st of year. But I'm glad you've taken to writing again. We're coming home but I don't believe it'll be before April 1st.

I just received letters from Aunt Annie, Lettie & Imy and they were trays beans. My account of October 4th was interesting?

That's nothing. Got better ones still if I don't forget them! I never rote you about my Boche cane I took away from a Boche Sgt. at St. Mihiel & carried all thru the Argonne. The most wonderful yet insignificant 50 cent solace & help at nite, in dark & in the mud, or how it was shot out of my hand by a machine gun bullet; or—you remember cigarette case Aunt Ray gave me. I carried it religiously in my left breast pocket. Just had sort of a hunch. A bullet hit it rite at top edge & put spring on bum so it won't stay closed, also dented it or rather just bent over the edge; or [how] piece of shrapnel broke button on leg of trousers at St. Mihiel; or being sniped at by Boche artillery for half an hour (a battery actually fired at 2 of us for that length of time & we were only ones anywhere nearby); or ordering an Engineer Captain to arm his men and get them up a hill to assist against a Boche counter attack after a General (only with one star) had asked my advice on what to do when his Bn. commanders sent word back they couldn't hold out, etc. etc. It was a nice quiet branch—but I'd do it again, but at the same time, mind ye, je suis tres content la guerre finis.

It is an established fact that I was recommended for D.S.C., but the general—who never got very close to the seat of action, thot otherwise.

*Going to mess.*
*Lots of Love.*

# APPENDIX


## PERSONAL EXPERIENCE REPORT

### Of 1st Lt. Harvey L. Harris

## GENERAL HEADQUARTERS

American Expeditionary Forces
Office of Chief of Tank Corps

4 December 1918.

From:     The Chief of Tank Corps, American E. F.
To:       All officers of the Tank Corps, American E. F.
Subject:  Personal Experience Reports.

1. The Chief of Tank Corps, American E. F. desires that the brilliant exploits of the Tank Corps shall be recorded, not simply by the bare record of dates and facts as appears in the War Diaries and Operation Reports, but also by narratives of personal experiences giving a much clearer and more vivid idea of the splendid achievements of the Corps. He feels that this is not only to the best interests of the Corps but is also due the families and friends at home. Particularly is this true in the case of the families and friends of those brave companions in arms who have so gallantly given their lives in the cause of liberty.

2. In view of the fact that the personnel of the present Tank Corps organization is subject to almost daily changes, which might render the desired information unavailable, a narrative of his personal experiences in the American E. F. is requested of every Tank Officer in France. Those narratives will be forwarded in duplicate, thru military channels, to the Assistant Chief of Staff, G-3, Headquarters Tank Corps, American E. F., without unnecessary delay.

3. The narrative should cover the important features of each officer's experience in France; should ordinarily be not longer than 1000 words; should contain all possible local color and human interest; should be written in the second person, giving all facts which might ordinarily be withheld on account of modesty; should also mention commendable acts of others witnessed by the writer. A vivid, interesting story is desired, not a report.

4. All organization commanders will take the necessary steps to expedite the preparation and forwarding of these narratives.

By command of Brigadier General ROCKENBACH:

*GEORGE J. CROSBY,*
*Major, Tank Corps,*
*Adjutant*

HQS., 331ST BN., TANK CORPS,

Varennes, France,
19 December 1918.

From:    1st Lt. Harvey L. Harris, Tank Corps, U. S. A.
To:    Assistant Chief of Staff, G-3, Hqs., Tank Corps,
    A.E.F. (Thru Military Channels.)

Subject:    Personal Experience Report.

1. In compliance with request of the Chief of Tank Corps, American Expeditionary Forces, dated 4 December, 1918, 1st Lt. Harvey L. Harris, 331st Battalion, Tank Corps, submits the following narrative of personal experience in the American Expeditionary Forces:

### "A DAY WITH THE TANKS IN THE ARGONNE"

Every time I look out of my window here I see a ridge which is the old valley wall of the now insignificant Aire River. It is about 400 meters from Varennes and, by looking more determinedly, I can see the very place our tanks laid under its protection. We were there for two nights, i.e., the nights of September 27th and 28th. On the morning of the 29th, with the 35th Division having awfully hard going South and Southwest of Charpentry, we were ordered up to assist. I'd been up most of the night before and felt pretty rotten. At 4. A.M. we started to get ready. Our Mess Sergeant had been up since 1 A.M. Water for coffee had to be carried from foot of bridge here at Varennes, etc. At 6 we had coffee in the rain, and dark and gloomy. I felt better but was too busy looking after the tanks of my platoon to do much damning of the Boche for making us get into the war. Just before leaving a lieutenant stuck a bottle of something at me—"Boche Cognac!"

About 200 meters from juncture of National Highway, I could see that the Boche were shelling the junction with G.I. cans. A Captain, whom I knew was on staff of 35th Division, stopped me and said, "Thank God, we can't advance on account of machine guns." It wouldn't have made any difference to him if opposition was 420's. He'd have wanted our little tanks to clean them up anyway. It's surprising what they ask us to do. Doughboys to Generals have sent us against places a battleship couldn't capture, but that's all outside the story. "There are snipers along the road. You'd better get in your tank," he cautioned. I walked a little further and saw a couple of doughboys go down—then decided to get aboard. It isn't an easy matter for me to get into the tank through those two small rear doors even when in training—let alone with haversack, pistol, belt, etc. I was hung up for a while but got in and lumbered down the road. There didn't seem to be anything going on so I climbed out and sat just back of turret, my feet hanging inside and my body almost entirely protected in front by the turret. I passed the General and his Staff sitting in a gully at the side of the road. I'll never forget the appreciative "You're the man we're waiting for" expression as I rode by. This look did more to thrill me than words could possibly have done.

And still nothing stirring! As we approached this junction though, things warmed up. The Boche weren't more than 500 meters away with their 77's and 88's and they know the importance of shelling roads! I was jarred several times from concussions of exploding shells. Then I noticed my C.O. at side of road (I spoke above of General and staff in gully 3 ft. deep at edge of road.) When one speaks of a General's P.C. (Hqs.) he often imagines the "old man" is in a bomb proof shelter, orderlies running around, telephones ringing and the fight miles up ahead. Not so in this war! I haven't seen a Brigade yet but what the General was up in front and his P.C. wherever he happened to be: along road or in a shell hole.

He motioned for me to pull tanks over behind a hedge—which I did, and camouflaged them as best I could. But they'd been heard rumbling along. It would be lucky if they weren't hit. But they weren't although whizz-bangs, the kind you don't hear until they hit, came all around them all afternoon until the batteries that were firing had to withdraw. With artillery hidden and firing at your tanks, the only thing to do is hide yourself and them.

After the tanks were camouflaged I went with my Captain, several other lieutenants and the men to a gully nearby. This gully ran out into Aire valley and, after we'd settled down to an all afternoon wait, I decided to see what I could by going to the edge of this gully and looking across the Aire valley about 1500 meters. There I was safe from every shell and, looking out across the river to the flats on the other side, could see two companies of tanks advancing in line, infantry following at several hundred meters—just as pretty as the shows we'd put on at Bourg for Staff School. At the far edge of the flats was the east edge of the Argonne. Everything seemed to be going well until a shell exploded amidst the infantry. Then another in front of advancing tanks; then another to the right. The doughboys immediately flopped down and the tanks continued, not knowing it. Then I saw a puff of smoke where forest sort of jutted towards me and a shell exploded within ten feet of a tank. Several turned for a depression near river, the others went for the woods, not knowing where the shots were coming from. And there I sat unable to do a thing, probably the only one who knew where those guns were—the flash had told me. With the aid of glasses I could actually see the Boche gun-crew working, loading, and if my voice would have carried, I could have yelled the instant the #1 (man who fires the piece) had his hand on grip and was going to fire. But that was out of the question. I thought of firing over at it with a 37 mm—from a tank—but probably wouldn't get within hundreds of yards. The range was, I should say, 2000 meters. Too much for a 37.

What to do? It was getting late. In half an hour it would be dusk. The doughboys, I could faintly make out, were digging in. The tanks were in the woods and might come any moment directly in front of the battery (for by this time I had been able to make out at least three guns) and be blown to pieces. Something had to be done damned quick.

I looked around and a captain and two enlisted men were approaching my point of vantage which was darned good for an observation point. The men carried wire and field phones. As the captain came neared, I saw his crossed cannons and, before I could say a word, he said, "I'm going to set up our forward P.C. here. My battery is just back there a ways. See anything to shoot at?" "Well, I'll be damned," was all I could say, and pointed across the valley. What had sent him there at that minute? Three minutes later I probably would have gone back to the place I'd left the Captain, and he might not have seen the battery as it was fast getting dark.

Then I "came out of it" in a fraction of a second and told him the whole story. Meanwhile he'd ordered a phone rigged up from the battery. While waiting for this connection he set up his telescope and figured out the data, etc. "Hurry, hurry, hurry! In ten minutes we won't be able to see a thing 100 yards away," I thought to myself.

"Hello. Yes, this is Captain (I don't remember his name). Is Lt. _____

there? Take this data. Work fast. Range 2200, (deflection something else) H.E. Sweeping." Four reports and they whistled over us. Four flashes, I estimated a couple of hundred yards short or target. "2600" and he kicked up the range 400. They were lost in woods. "They ought to be worried by now," he said, (the deflection was OK) "2400, 3 rounds on 2nd piece close 5"—and 12 of 'em went over us, and 3 at least landed right at that corner of woods. "That's got 'em. I saw two guns get direct hits. The crews must be finished, too." And it got dark so that we could hardly see the valley directly below us.

"'You've done something today, Captain," I said. "Wasn't that fine?" he answered.

I went back to tanks and found that a runner had been looking for me for an hour. Most of the tanks had already gone back behind the hill towards Varennes. What a different night I spent to the preceding two! It was still cold, wet and raining—but I was warm within. "Tomorrow I'll show him that observation tower near Apremont. Some more good fun," I thought as I sat on the running board of our Mack truck (the inside and underneath crowded with enlisted men) and went to sleep as best I could.

# BIBLIOGRAPHY

Henry Berry. *Make the Kaiser Dance.* Garden City, N.Y.: Doubleday & Company, 1978.

Edward M. Coffman. *The War to End All Wars. The American Military Experience in World War I.* Madison: University of Wisconsin Press, 1986.

Carlo D'Este. *Patton. A Genius for War.* New York: HarperCollins Publishers, Inc., 1995.

Samuel Hynes.*The Soldiers' Tale. Bearing Witness to Modern War.* New York: Viking Penguin, 1997.

Robert E. Rogge. "The 304th Tank Brigade. Its Formation and First Two Actions," *Armor*, July–August, 1988, 26–34.

Dale E. Wilson. *Treat 'Em Rough! The Birth of American Armor, 1917–1920.* Novato, California: Presidio Press, 1989.

**TANK CORPS**

**TREAT EM' ROUGH**

The letters written by Harvey Harris are retained by family members. The quotation of then Lt. Col. George S. Patton, Jr., referred to on page ix and repeated on the back cover, was contained in a letter of Harvey Harris to his nephew, Frank Harris, dated April 18, 1944.

# LIST OF ILLUSTRATIONS